Dear Miss Baird

A Portrait of a 19th-Century Family

Dear Miss
Baird

A Portrait of a 19th-Century Family

Elizabeth Nussbaum

THE CHARLBURY PRESS
OXFORDSHIRE

ISBN 0 9546342 0 9

A catalogue record for this book is available from the British Library

This edition first published by The Charlbury Press, November 2003

Printed in the United Kingdom by The Alden Press, Oxford. This publication is printed on acid-free paper

The Charlbury Press, Orchard Piece, Crawborough, Charlbury, Oxfordshire OX7 3TX, UK

The Charlbury Press is an imprint of Day Books, **www.day-books.com**

Contents

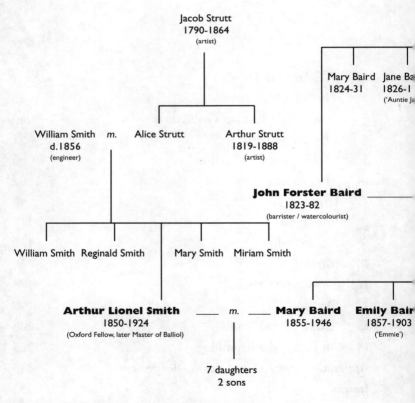

Frances Potts   Anne Potts   Mary Potts
1797-1856

Jacob Strutt
1790-1864
(artist)

Mary Baird   Jane Ba
1824-31   1826-1
('Auntie Ja

William Smith   m.   Alice Strutt   Arthur Strutt
d.1856   1819-1888
(engineer)   (artist)

John Forster Baird
1823-82
(barrister / watercolourist)

William Smith Reginald Smith   Mary Smith Miriam Smith

Arthur Lionel Smith   ___ m. ___   Mary Baird   Emily Bair
1850-1924   1855-1946   1857-1903
(Oxford Fellow, later Master of Balliol)   ('Emmie')

7 daughters
2 sons

(Only those characters mentioned in the book are here.
Names in Bold indicate the authors of the original material used.)

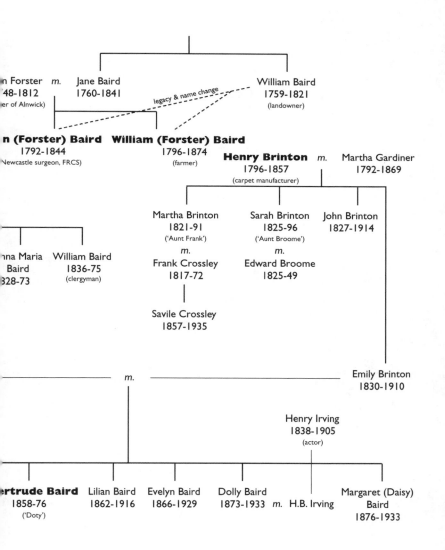

n Forster _m._ Jane Baird
48-1812   1760-1841
er of Alnwick)

                                    legacy & name change

William Baird
1759-1821
(landowner)

n (Forster) Baird   William (Forster) Baird
1792-1844   1796-1874
Newcastle surgeon, FRCS)   (farmer)

Henry Brinton _m._ Martha Gardiner
1796-1857   1792-1869
(carpet manufacturer)

Martha Brinton   Sarah Brinton   John Brinton
1821-91   1825-96   1827-1914
('Aunt Frank')   ('Aunt Broome')
_m._   _m._
Frank Crossley   Edward Broome
1817-72   1825-49

Savile Crossley
1857-1935

nna Maria   William Baird
Baird   1836-75
328-73   (clergyman)

                                    Emily Brinton
                                    1830-1910

                          _m._

Henry Irving
1838-1905
(actor)

rtrude Baird   Lilian Baird   Evelyn Baird   Dolly Baird   Margaret (Daisy)
1858-76   1862-1916   1866-1929   1873-1933 _m._ H.B. Irving   Baird
('Doty')   1876-1933

BAIRD FAMILY TREE

To
Daniel, Rosa, Giulio,
Max, Noah and Kim

1   The Angel of Death

The angel of death arrives
And I spring joyfully up
No one knows what comes over me
When I and that messenger speak.
     (From the Rubaiyat of Jalal al-din Rumi,
     13th century)

On a sunny morning at the end of April 1876 a young girl lay
dying at her home in Teddington, Surrey. She was 17 years old.
As her parents leant over her to lift the tangle of hair from her
damp forehead, she moved her head as if trying to shield them
from her infected breath. Outside the window, the first sunlight
was glinting on the leaves of the creeper; the dawn chorus from
the garden promised a fine day. But the watchers by the bed –
mother, father and hired nurse – were oblivious of this. The
family doctor had been summoned as dawn broke: and from the
way that this hardened medical man, who had witnessed
countless deaths, wept as he stood at the foot of the bed, they
knew there was no hope.

The dying girl was Gertrude Alice Baird. She was the third
daughter of Emily and John Forster Baird of Woodlands,
Teddington. A year earlier she had been sent away to boarding
school in Hove. In her final term there, just before she was due
to leave, she had caught whooping-cough, and then developed

1

measles after she came home. Diphtheria two weeks later was the finishing touch. Three of the merciless 19th-century killer diseases in the space of two months was more than most constitutions could withstand.

She was only one of the thousands of young people who died of diphtheria that year. The epidemic had raged through England. Diphtheria was a particularly unpleasant disease. A false membrane grew across the throat, stifling breath, and as the illness developed it affected the muscles of the heart. Only the fit and strong could resist it. This young girl was neither.

Her funeral was held four days later in the square-towered 16th-century church of St Mary's, nestling at the bottom of Teddington's High Street within sight of the river. As the procession wound down the road, shopkeepers put up their shutters and drew their curtains out of respect for the family. The women of a family often stayed away from funerals in the 19th century, but this was an intimate family affair and four of Gertrude's five sisters attended. The youngest, a little two-year-old, trotted to the grave and threw in a posy of spring blossom on top of the wreaths and bunches of flowers. Only Gertrude's eldest sister Mary, and her mother, were absent: Mary in bed with measles, her mother looking after her.

This is the bare outline of what was a nodal event in the life of the Bairds. They were a large, typically Victorian family – a typical middle-class family, that is. Like many big families they lived with a self-centred delight in the things they did, which made them attractive not only to themselves but to outsiders as well. It also made them prolific journal- and letter-writers; and the screeds of letters triggered by Gertrude Baird's death were all lovingly preserved by her contemporaries and passed on to their descendants, of whom I am one.

Mary, Gertrude's sister and the eldest Baird daughter, was my grandmother. She was the longest-lived in her generation; and my mother, Mary's eighth child, was the longest-lived of hers (both died at 91). It is largely due to this accident and a process of what one might call family gravity that this hoard of documents has descended to me and is now sitting in boxes in my study. There are letters, journals, account-books, stories, plays, sketchbooks and photographs – a patchwork record of nearly a century in the life of one family. Looking at them you begin to feel that this family had more energy than could ever be contained within the limits of everyday life and the surplus overflowed into all these notebooks. But of course what they really had a surplus of was time. Most servanted middle-class families wrote and drew. What makes this collection remarkable is that it has survived largely intact; and that is due to that early morning scene in Teddington when the 17-year-old Gertrude lay on her deathbed.

Minutes before she died, in fact almost at the moment of death, Gertrude had a vision. It was similar to a near-death experience, only in this case it was a death experience. It electrified those who witnessed it. It seemed for a minute to have torn the veil separating the here and now from the beyond: the onlookers had virtually seen her cross over. The sense of specialness that the family had always had was enhanced by her dying vision and her words, or her 'song' as the family called it afterwards: and anything connected with her came to be invested with a special aura. The collections of letters in their leather bindings began, and any family relic from that period acquired a feeling of sanctity. Gertrude, without knowing it, had become the muse of family history. Cut off before she herself could have any children, she unwittingly spawned a cult. And her eldest sister, the fecund Mary, prolific diarist and mother-to-be of nine, carried on the good work. It is Mary's journals that this book focuses on, and Mary's account of her sister's death that I quote in this chapter. The manner of Gertrude's dying amazed her whole family; Mary's description of it amazes us, nearly 130 years later.

Mary to me was simply 'Granny', a formidable black-skirted person who lived alone with her maid and had knobbly fingers that could suddenly point at you as you struggled to answer unnerving questions like: 'What have you got to say for yourself?' (Nothing!) Now, ageing myself, I know that somewhere inside those black folds a young Mary still nestled, a spirited 20-year-old with cornflower-blue eyes, fair hair and a charm that drew young men to her like moths to a light. She had unusual social confidence, was highly intelligent, patchily educated (at home by governesses – seven in her first 12 years), bossy to her siblings and the bane of her manipulative mother.

But tensions in the family were leavened by a lot of fun and family loyalties were strong, cemented as they were by their sense of specialness. Private tribulations were usually kept for the pages of their journals. Mary wrote fluently (her handwriting courses across the page), with plentiful underlinings. The sisters, as far as I can judge, did not read each other's diaries. They might weep with fury and frustration, but they were not sneaky. And this raised a problem when I came to read their writings: I had a sense of eavesdropping. Here was I, a junior granddaughter (albeit now in my 60s) of an awesome if deceased grandmother, using her teenage diaries and letters to pry into the past. When I opened her and my grandfather's love-letters it felt even sneakier.

Then the very past I was exploring came, thankfully, to my rescue. (The past is not so much a foreign country as an infallibly safe one, for onlookers at least.) In my treasure trove was a letter written in 1819 on paper as thin as gossamer and crossed (written first in one direction and then across it on the same page to minimize the cost of postage) from my great-great-grandfather, one Henry Brinton, to his future wife, Martha Gardiner of Dublin. A love-letter. And – this is where the ghosts of the past came to my help – a great-aunt, my grandmother's youngest sister Daisy who was born a few months after Gertrude's death, had transcribed it. So not only did I have a crib; my conscience was salved. If my great-aunt could eavesdrop, so could I.

The family records in my possession go back to this period, the 1820s. This book is not a chronological account, rather a series of scenarios, a ferreting into one burrow after another according to what my diggings produce and what those boxes hold. Gertrude's death remains the key point, not just for her family but for me too. It was Gertrude's death that first made me interested in history by giving me a sense of my personal link with it. This moment of awareness – of the thread that connects subjective present to objective past – is for ever associated in my mind with the smell of roast beef: lunch at Granny's, when a kind of nerves might make me gag on the greens but after lunch brought the rich reward of looking at Great-Aunt Gertrude's pictures. The album of her teenage paintings would be brought out and reverently we (the grandchildren were always paired) would turn the pages. We were not sure whether or not she had been a genius; the pictures of witches about to be burnt, woodland goblins and ghosts listening in at nursery story-time were morbidly fun to our 20th-century eyes. But the main thing was that Gertrude had died young, not old like most of the family. Seventeen was an age that we ourselves could envisage being; and at her death extraordinary things had happened which our parents described, as theirs had, in a special tone of voice that sent shivers up your spine.

So this story begins with the death of Gertrude; one Victorian schoolgirl among the many whose families did not know quite what to do with them, but felt they should encourage their talents in an age when women's education was beginning (just) to be seen as a social asset. One thing we can be sure they never thought about was the health risk she ran, cooped up with twenty other teenagers. They had apparently not read *Jane Eyre*. In any case, notions of infection were slow to catch on. Five years earlier Lister had successfully demonstrated the effectiveness of carbolic acid in the fight against bacteria, but in London hospitals doctors could still get a laugh out of their students by telling them to shut the door 'to keep Mr Lister's germs out'.

The Bairds waited ten days after Gertrude went to bed with measles before they decided to move the other children out into lodgings in Teddington. Four of the daughters – Emily (or Emmie as I shall call her and as she was later known, to avoid confusion with her mother who was also an Emily), Lilian, Evelyn and Dolly, aged 18, 14, nine and two respectively – were put in the charge of their father's sister, Jane Baird (Auntie Jane) and farmed out. Twenty-year-old Mary stayed in the house; she had to be kept away from the younger children because she too had developed what looked suspiciously like a diphtherial throat. That, at least, was what they were told. But from this distance one can see a different motive. No one had minded much about the risk of infection for nearly a fortnight. Now there was a more sombre reason to clear the house of young ones.

It is hard today to recapture the atmosphere that must have prevailed in a Victorian home at moments like this. To the parents it must have seemed that the old man with the scythe was making a deliberate swipe at them as all the children except Emmie went down with one or more of these diseases. Their doctor, Mr Holberton, adopted the fatalistic attitude of his age, the only treatment for diphtheria at the time being palliative: tracheotomy or bypassing the false membrane or cauterisation of the larynx (burning with a hot iron or caustic substance) which was used on Mary later.

He had been summoned on the day Gertrude woke up with spots and a fever, Mary reported in her diary: 'April 17, G awoke very spotty. . . . At 1.0 Mr Holberton came and pronounced it measles, but said it would be foolish to take any precautions, though Emmie and Lilian are the only two that have had it.' Not surprisingly the rest of the children did get measles, including Mary, which prevented her from going to her sister's funeral. Before that she had helped nurse two-year-old Dolly who had whooped all night (Dolly's crib had been moved into Mary's room), 'coughing and waking up every ¼ of an hour'. Four days later Mary's sore throat developed. 'They cauterised [it] very effectively, pronouncing it a patch of the true diphtheria sort, but adding that it could quite well be stopped when the person was in health, which I am.' Her throat was cauterized again two days later, and on what was the eve of Gertrude's death (though she did not know it) it was 'burnt again with nitrate of silver'. Our eyes water at the thought, but Mary was stoical: 'Naturally my throat felt sore from the burning and my head ached a little, but I am very nearly all right again.'

Before we follow Mary's account any further I want to turn to the 1871 census to get a bird's-eye view of that Baird household in their Teddington home. Their house, Woodlands, is still standing (though it is no longer called that): a typical three-storey Victorian house in Hampton Road, about five minutes' walk from Bushey Park. It was built not long before the Bairds took out a renewable lease on it in 1870. It is a stout, roomy house – and it needed to be. At the time of the 1871 census it housed thirteen people.

John F. Baird, then aged 48, was listed as 'head'. He gave his profession as barrister and landowner but we, his great-grandchildren, know better. Landowner yes, in Northumberland where he was born; but he is remembered for his lifetime devotion to watercolour painting rather than for his barristering. But you cannot put 'gifted amateur painter' on a census form, so 'barrister', which he was intermittently, did instead. At the time of the census he was in good health, a well-built bearded man with a reserved look in his thoughtful eyes and an outwardly easy-going nature. By the end of the decade the shadow of the tuberculosis which was to kill him was creeping up.

Next comes Emily J. Baird, his wife, aged 40. As mother to (then) five daughters and organizer of three servants, one German governess, a gardener and various visiting tutors she had a busy life with frequent servant problems – the stresses of opulence, one might call it. But there were other sides to Emily, as we shall see. Her health was excellent, in spite of a tendency towards neuralgia, and she lived into the 20th century. She had great reserves of physical energy and expressive blue eyes that could sparkle with amusement but more often were frowning with disapproval at the behaviour of one of her daughters, particularly her eldest. These daughters were Mary, aged 15 at the time of the census; Emmie, 14; Gertrude, 12; Lilian, eight, and Evelyn four. (Dolly, the two-year-old with whooping-cough, was born three years later.) The census quaintly lists them all as 'scholars', even four-year-old Evelyn. With roughly 18 months separating the first three girls, then a four-year gap before the next was born, there were in effect two families, an upper and lower nursery. It is with the upper family that this book is concerned: Mary, who at the time of the census had the innocent fair-haired sheen of an apprentice angel, belied by a sharp wit and compulsive flirtatiousness; Emmie, who had chosen amenability as her role; and Gertrude who felt or had been told she was plain (looks mattered a lot to the Bairds) and who took refuge in an inner world of creativity. These then were the older 'scholars' on the census, whose only link with scholarship so far had been a succession of governesses and their mother's stern tutelage. These are the three girls at the centre of this story, and it is their diaries and letters and (in Gertrude's case) stories which enable us to see into their inner lives.

Census day in autumn 1871 also saw visitors at the house: Frances Potts, John Forster Baird's Northumbrian aunt (his mother's sister), aged 66, is listed as 'assistant', as is Jane Baird (Auntie Jane), his 44-year-old sister from Northumberland. Knowing Emily Baird's short temper and her sometimes less than warm feelings towards her sister-in-law Jane, one can imagine the tension that little triangle of elder women might generate. It is hinted at in the diaries.

Then there are the servants: Mathilda Frick, the 19-year-old German governess from Kaiserslautern in Bavaria; Elizabeth White, 41, the cook from a village near Loughborough; Charlotte Bell, 29, the housemaid from London; Emma Bain, 30, the parlourmaid from Somerleyton in Suffolk. Each of these entries tells a story that is woven into the family's history. Mathilda had been recruited on family travels in Germany, Emma from the household of a wealthy sister-in-law in Suffolk. Mathilda (Thilda to the family) became a close friend to Emmie, finally leaving Teddington in the mid-1870s for another family from where she visited the Bairds, bearing the unmistakable tell-tale symptoms of tuberculosis (again, nobody worried about infection).

These, then, are some of the cast of characters who five years later were present during that unfolding family tragedy in the spring of 1876. Frances Potts had gone but Auntie Jane was back again, the archetypal Victorian maiden aunt ever on hand in a crisis. Only Emmie and her parents managed to avoid any of the infections. Each of the younger children, though finally removed from the house, caught (and survived) one or other of them. And the Bairds were a privileged family: they never missed meals, they ate fresh fruit and vegetables, went for long walks, and lived in a large airy house. It is not hard to imagine the ravages that could occur in the absence of such advantages. (In the 1850s over 28,000 children and young adults had died of diphtheria; 20 years later the disease peaked again, and it was this epidemic that caught Gertrude.)

Mary at first took a typically healthy 20-year-old's attitude to the family ills. Although her infection and its treatment must have caused her considerable pain she did not complain. Serious illness was still something that happened to other people. The major preoccupations in her diary were matters of the heart, and religion. She began the diary on April 5th 1876 with the solemn subtitle: 'My Times are in Thy Hands'. By making this dedication she was grounding her journal in the faith that informed her whole life.

Piety, religion and church were things she had grown up with. Her father was an accepting, uncritical member of the Church of England; her mother, who came from a Quaker background, had adopted her husband's Anglicanism. In the small Teddington community, church affairs occupied a large part of every Sunday and spilled over into the week with social events and entertaining between the families who shared this devotional bond. It is difficult to comprehend from the distance of our sceptical century the extent to which the church provided a social as well as religious framework for the lives of its adherents – this in the aftermath of the low-church revivalism and the Oxford movement that had polarized the country in the middle years of the century.

Church-going was a central part of Mary's life, for several reasons. First, she regularly taught at Sunday school, which she loved; secondly, it gave her the solace and comfort she needed in her battles with her conscience and in dealing with the frustrations of family life, all minutely recorded in her diary; and lastly it provided one of the venues for her endless *affaires de cœur*. The Sunday services offered a heaven-sent opportunity to meet your latest admirer and conduct a covert flirtation while he escorted you home.

Her opening entry on that April 5th takes us straight into Teddington life. In the morning she met local friends and made arrangements for going to the Boat Race the following Saturday with one Jack Barton, a neighbour and the current escort. She then 'parished' (visited the poor), 'unsuccessfully, I fear, as I could not induce a mother to bring her 6 children [one of whom was in Mary's Sunday school class] to Baptism'. The following day she was planning a family dance, fixed for the 25th, with her mother. A letter arrived from her 18-year-old cousin, Savile Crossley of Somerleyton Hall (where the parlourmaid had been recruited). Savile, friend and bosom-confidant of two years earlier, was currently exploring in other directions but the two were still very close. Later that day Mary was left in charge of the whooping-cough patients 'who are getting worse, not better, on the principle that things must be worse before they are better'. She decided it was good for her to have Dolly with her at night to teach her, Mary, patience: 'I have not the heart to scold her and it *is* irritating to be waked up for hours in the sleepiest time of night'; but she stroked Dolly's hot forehead and was rewarded by a kiss from the feverish child.

Saturday April 8th was Boat Race day, 'a most magnificent summer day, not a cloud from morning to night'. Not so nice, though, if you were wearing mourning. Her father's brother

William, a clergyman, had died the previous December. Mary felt it was her duty to keep on her 'dusty black' at least till Easter Sunday, still a week away. She travelled with her father, Emmie and Jack Barton by train from Teddington to Mortlake, then walked to the river. The Oxford and Cambridge Boat Race was a great social event, with the river bank thronged with spectators. 'There we stood,' Mary wrote, 'in the glare and broil of the midday sun, and almost choked with dust and tobacco.' Cambridge won. The family returned on foot via Kew Gardens and from there along the towpath to Richmond (they were stalwart walkers), 'two by two, I with J.B. . . . I was very happy, as I like Jack and have known him long enough to feel a pleasant safety in allowing myself to do so. . . . I don't think I flirted.' You can hear the note of doubt; and when Jack stayed for supper there was play between them over a sprig of heliotrope that Mary had picked, reminding her of a similar incident involving the previous year's (rejected) suitor, her neighhbour Jerry Burchell, who had told her the true meaning of the plant was '*je vous aime*'. Mary's diaries provide many such glimpses of the ritual flirtation that marked the long process leading up to Victorian marriage.

Three days later Gertrude returned from school. She looked 'very ill, so blue and thin'. Mary has a gift for the telling phrase. Reading this one's heart sinks; but Mary reassured herself. Gertrude would soon pick up, not get the measles which she knew had broken out at Madame Collinet's, as the school was known, after the name of its owner.

The weather suddenly changed, typical of April, with snow and sleet the next day, Maundy Thursday. 'Church as usual in the evening. Vicar preached, also as usual,' Mary recorded tersely. The next day Gertrude was very poorly, which kept her but not Mary and Emmie from church. The two eldest girls went to the Good Friday three-hour service, then later to Evensong; about five hours of church in all. But 'as the Vicar did the Meditations we could not feel very devotional, which was a pity. . . . How I wish I could keep my Lents and Good Fridays better.' This is a constant theme in Mary's diary, what one might call the battle, never completely resolved, between faith and fun.

Easter Sunday was the perfect fusion of the two: 'as pleasant an Easter as any I have spent here,' Mary reported – this in spite of a bad night with Dolly. Gertrude, feeling better, went to early service but 'seemed, and looked very seedy'. Mary taught her Sunday-school pupils, twelve of them, bringing them home with her afterwards for Easter eggs. She was out of mourning now, wearing a new bonnet, 'a turn-up-in-front shape of common straw, trimmed with black velvet and corn lace & feather . . . rather vulgar after my beloved black things'. At Evensong she bumped into Jerry Burchell, the rejected suitor, and felt a pang of remorse (helped by stony looks from his sister) at seeing how unhappy he looked. That night Mr Holberton was called to see Gertrude. He prescribed a warm bath and bed.

The next day, April 17th, the diagnosis of measles was announced. The family dance would have to be postponed, to Mary's chagrin. 'Alas! How I groaned inwardly, but I daresay that is the least of the consequences of Gertrude's foolish rashness, in saying good-bye to her sick school fellows' – there had evidently been much farewell embracing at the school. That afternoon Mary, Emmie and Jack Barton took a train to Surbiton and rambled in woods 'carpeted with lovely wood anemones and splendid primroses, all in perfection of bloom'. Jack Barton accompanied her home. 'He was very good to me (only that though) all day.' Mary speaks as an experienced flirt.

At some point during this first phase of Gertrude's illnesses at home her father sat beside his ailing daughter and together they drew up a list of the important events and dates in her life; a list that was kept by her mother and later folded into a bound collection of her husband's letters. With hindsight they have a horrifically terminal feel, those two pages beginning: '1858 Oct 4 Doty [Gertrude's nickname] born' and ending: '1876 Home. School. Home, illness.' But one can imagine the scene, father sitting beside the bed, pad and pencil in hand while they recall the key events of the previous 17 years: the foreign holidays, the trips to Northumberland, the sisters' births, their various house moves. Each entry would have its anecdotes and memories – good therapy for a sick child, and a boon for the biographer, with its list of their nomadic comings and goings.

But whatever ruses the parents thought up to cheer the patient, things were rapidly, ineluctably getting worse. The weather had in fact improved: 'Easter Tuesday. Today has been a rather pleasant "growy" spring day, much warmer with soft rains,' Mary recorded, but in spite of that she felt low-spirited. She was not allowed to teach her 'beloved S.S.' (Sunday school); she was needed at home, and perhaps more important, 'Mama and I are for the thousandth time on "ungood" terms'. Everyone was in and out of Gertrude's room. Mama and Emmie 'read to her all day, and ask her perpetual questions'. Mary (nose a little out of joint?) is tartly critical. 'If I catch this illness my one desire will be to be left alone, no reading, talkings, starings or questions.'

Her moods chase each other across the page. She was incubating two of these diseases herself, so it is not surprising she felt off-colour. There is a three-day gap in the diary. By the following Friday Gertrude had developed a 'dreadful throat'. Mr Holberton, 'very grave', gave evasive answers to her father's string of questions, 'perhaps because he knows how extremely

14

nervous Papa is'. There was another shifting of beds as Gertrude was moved into her parents' room. Mary wanted to get Gertrude prayed for in the church, an idea which appalled Emmie, the only person she dared mention it to, but she nonetheless planned to sneak down and ask the vicar. A spat with her mother about reading to Gertrude put her in a really bad mood (she had offered to read aloud to Gertrude, then their mother criticized her in some unspecified way and she had left the room). 'Everyone seems to be quite out of their minds with this illness. . . . Papa came down green, ate no dinner, and upon that went off to get a horrid nurse for G. I am writing in an undutiful strain, but I did feel so angry at being so treated.'

On the following Sunday Gertrude was prayed for in church. Old sores were forgotten as Jerry Burchell came over to Mary after church and took her hand. Her father appeared at the church door, looking for a member of the congregation who was said to have the address of another doctor, and Mary grasped for the first time how serious the situation was. The combination of Jerry's solicitude and her father's desperation nearly undid her, she reports; 'however, kind sympathisers soon crowded round me and walked home with me'. Later in the day her old self reasserted itself when friends came to take her for a walk in Bushey Park. One of them, Freddy Johnson, 'tried to enter into a vigorous flirtation with me, quite in the old style, which amused and enlivened me much'. Flirting was the green fuse which again and again kept her spirits high: and now she needed its help more than ever before.

During the night Gertrude had 'coughed up thick pieces of "false membrane" which show the disease to have spread dangerously further'. In spite of that, Mary reported that Dr Johnson, the new doctor, had told them there was still more to hope for than to fear. One wonders if he really believed it.

15

That was Sunday evening, April 23rd. By the following Tuesday, Mary was having her own throat cauterized. The children had been banned from the sickroom. Only parents, doctors, Auntie Jane and the nurse were allowed in. The nurse had turned out to be surprisingly sympathetic, in spite of Mary's fears: 'She is the nicest creature, and *good* too. She looks so appetizing, in her white cap with long lappets, check print dress and white apron.' Then on the Wednesday evening, Mr Holberton announced that Gertrude had taken a turn for the better: an opinion confirmed the following morning by Dr Johnson.

Meanwhile parents and nurse tending the patient were desperately trying to contain the infection. 'The smell of the incessant discharges from her chest is very offensive, so that they can hardly keep the room sweet; it is the most dangerously infectious part of the complaint,' Mary noted. That was when the young ones were evacuated. Mary alone remained at home, on the doctor's orders; not, as she first assumed, because of her infection, but (this was written several days later) 'out of consideration to our parents, leaving them a daughter as a consolation'.

'The dear child has almost ceased to take any notice of what goes on,' she wrote a day later. Gertrude was still obediently taking her food: beef-tea and wine, this last making her cry out with the pain it caused her throat. Mr Holberton, tending Mary for her nitrate-of-silver treatment, told her he was going to put turpentine on Gertrude's chest to 'numb the pain'. Mary commented: 'It didn't strike me that this "numbing" meant other than perhaps cure.' Told to sleep, Mary obeyed. She added another retrospective comment: 'All day [Friday] I was very poorly & hardly seemed to notice everyone's fears with regard to our darling; but they also hid them from me.'

She woke at 9 a.m. the following morning, Saturday April 29th, to find her mother standing beside her, red-eyed. Mary asked how Gertrude was.

She [her mother] said, 'She is more comfortable.' 'Is she better?' 'No, darling.' 'Has Papa fetched Dr Johnson?' 'No, it's no use.' 'What do you mean?' I said, then I caught something in her eye, and cried out, while Mama threw her arms about me, and said that our darling was 'singing the praises of the Lamb'. Then I fell among the clothes, and cried so long, but not loudly, after Mama said it was sacrilege to disturb the sleep of such happy dead.

She had slept through her sister's death. Perhaps because of that, anxious not to lose a single detail of it, she wrote a minute description of it in her diary compiled from the nurse's eye-witness account and presumably from what her parents told her. Mary's account became a sort of gospel. It was copied to friends, who then recopied it and sent it back for other members of the family who might not have seen it.

Her parents had left the sickroom and gone to sleep, on that Friday/Saturday night, for a couple of hours. When they came back they saw a change in Gertrude's condition and sent for Mr Holberton. He, quite overcome, knowing that nothing could be done, leant on the end of the bed.

'Is there no hope?' her mother asked him. (This dialogue was reported by Mary.)

'None, I fear,' the doctor answered, words which Gertrude must have heard as a short time afterwards she clutched her mother's arm and asked: 'What did he say that for, what did he mean?'

Her mother: 'Are you afraid to die, darling?'

Gertrude: 'Oh no, not afraid, but this can't be dying, it's not like this. I have *so* much life in me.'

Her mother lay down beside her and read psalms and hymns,

while the doctor, unable to contain his emotions, left the room. There was another short interchange between mother and daughter in which Gertrude whispered the names of all the members of the family, sending them her love. Not long after that the nurse said: 'She's going.' Her mother leant over her to support her during her fight for breath. Then came what Mary called 'Gertrude's message' or 'her wondrous song'. Let Mary's words describe it:

A most eager, brilliant expression came into her face; her eyes shone, & she broke out into an ecstatic song, at first low, then her voice gained strength, her eyes still more bright, her face more eagerness. This is as far as I can collect of her wondrous song: 'They come! They come! I see angels – angels everywhere – they shout! They cry! So bright! So beautiful – they see the child – the child sees them – they weep – but the child does not weep. They come! They come! They sing! They shout! They cry: Glory to God in the Highest! The child sees them! – the child will come! – Oh God! Oh God! Glory! Glory! Glory to Thee, Great Father! Glory to Thee, Oh Son! Glory to the Holy One! Glory! Glory!' All this time she had a bright eager look, & she sprang forward in bed three times and covered her face with her hands as if what she saw was too bright to look upon. Then she sank back on her pillows & seemed to be calling Mama several times, a slight shiver passed through her frame & then she sank to rest. . . . During her song poor Mama, afraid lest she should exhaust her strength, whispered to Nurse: 'Can't you stop her?' & Nurse said 'Oh no Ma'am, she's not here.' Nurse heard nearly all, until her speech grew too rapid in her intense eagerness. Poor Mama was too grieved over the darling's bodily suffering to hear all, but indeed that suffering was very short. At the end, as she fell back, Papa read the Commendatory Prayer.

Mary concluded: 'Blessed are the pure in heart, for they shall see God – He leadeth me beside the Still Waters.' She added Gertrude's name and dates: 'Gertrude Alice Baird. Born October 4th 1858 – Died April 29th 1876 aged 17 years & 7 months. R.I.P.'

That same morning the exiled children returned. Mary

recorded how she and Emmie went upstairs with Auntie Jane, 'to look at (but oh! not even to touch) our dearest'.

There she lay, as if in a most reposeful slumber, her dear head, with that intellectual forehead shaded as in life by her hair, which Charlotte [the maid] had lovingly plaited on one side, her steadfast mouth, always so expressive, now telling us in language which we could well understand, of the peace and comfort of those 'Everlasting Arms' to which she was ready and eager to go. It was our Doty, 'my Doty' as poor Emmie said, and yet another Doty. . . . I felt a sanctifying influence pervading the house, which comes from that darkened room; and yet not purely from there.

Mary went up on her own several times. She laid lilies-of-the-valley on Gertrude's breast and said prayers, then sat in silence. 'Has our angel already left me some of the blessing she had on earth?' she asks in her diary. The last time she went into the room was with a photographer. 'I felt it almost sacrilege,' she confessed. But photography, a new toy, was becoming a part of life. And we can only be glad that on this occasion it was, for we still have that photograph. There is Gertrude lying peacefully, with her long plaited hair, looking indeed as she herself had said minutes before she died as if she has still so much life in her. The calm Mary evinces in her diary, which she was able to use that same evening when she talked to her mother about their beloved Doty and read aloud to her, must have derived in part from the feeling of disbelief one has after a death, and in this case the disbelief would have been reinforced by the 'sleeping' quality of Gertrude's repose. It is this quality that the camera has caught. Her eyes are closed, her head slightly tilted to one side; her face seems to show not the ravages of illness but the fullness of youth, with strong features whose beauty would have developed as they became marked by experience and time – the time she did not have.

John Forster Baird kept a set of pictures of his children in a leather wallet: seven children (the last, Daisy, was born four months after Gertrude's death – Emily never got her boy) and eight photographs. There are two of Gertrude, one of her alive and the other taken after her death.

I decided when I started work on this book to find out more about the near-death experiences I mentioned earlier. They are being researched by a number of people. I wrote to one of them, Dr Peter Fenwick of the Maudsley Hospital, describing Gertrude's death. He replied that he would categorize it as a mystical experience. In his book, *The Truth and the Light*, he elaborates on this type of near-death experience: 'These mystical experiences have always fascinated me because they seem to lie at the frontiers of science: we can find partial scientific explanations for them but they can't be explained entirely by the mechanisms we already know.'

The scientific explanation was summed up in a *Radio Times* review by Polly Toynbee in June 1998: 'Those who have a near-death experience see a tunnel of light and feel a surge of wellbeing. Bliss, one person calls it. A coming together of memory, meaning, happiness and reassurance. It is a neurological effect. . . . As oxygen leaves the brain neurons in the eye fire at random, producing bright light sensations, always brightest in the centre. Powerful opiates are suddenly released in the brain to relieve the extreme stress. These induce hallucinations and fire off parts of the brain connected to memory and emotion.'

But for the Bairds there was no doubt. The angels had come for their daughter. They had all but seen it themselves. It was no wonder her mother said that Gertrude was 'singing the praises of the Lamb'.

How they dealt with their loss, how the story of Mary and her swains, of her bereaved parents and their growing family continued we will look at later. At this point we will follow the documents back in time and explore the chain of events that led John Forster Baird of Newcastle and Emily Jane Brinton of Kidderminster to marry, then settle in Teddington; and find out why one of their daughters, out of so many, was chosen to be sent away to school.

2   *The John Generations*

My little Boy borne at 3 o'clock P.M.
John Baird, February 3rd 1823

It is perhaps lucky that the Bairds did not have a son. They would almost certainly have called him John, after John Forster Baird's father or his grandfather, and we would have four Johns to disentangle instead of three. Of the three we have, all are Forsters and two are Bairds as well. There is John Forster, draper, John Forster (a.k.a. Baird), surgeon, and John Forster Baird, the barrister–painter we know, Mary and Gertrude's father. They follow a direct line of descent – grandfather, father, son – with about 25 years between them each. The draper was born in the 1770s, the surgeon in the mid-1790s, his barrister-painter son, the 'little Boy' of the quotation above, in 1823.

John Forster Baird, the last of the three, is the one we his descendants know best. We speak of him as John-Forster-Baird (or Johnforsterbaird), a single four-syllable name which carries a powerful resonance. There is hardly a great-grandchild of his who does not have some of his paintings on their walls. Ironically, the very paintings he was shy of showing in his lifetime have earned him immortality; and with his pictures he has passed on a love of his county of origin, Northumberland. These comprise a potent legacy. When the script of some spiritualist automatic writings surfaced after my grandmother's death (she was fond of dabbling in the occult), purporting to be communications from John Forster Baird, we treated them with awe. He adjured his descendants to love Bamburgh, which it is not difficult to do. On the Northumbrian coast, 15 miles south of the Scottish border, it is a wild and beautiful place, easy to become addicted to, in spite of the weather. It was one of the homes of the Forster clan, and in the early 18th century they held its magnificent castle, then forfeited their claim to it in time to be on the wrong side in the first Jacobite rebellion (no great strategists, our ancestors). Those strange disjointed sentences in the 'communication' gave even the most sceptical of us pause for thought. Was this really John Forster Baird, speaking to us from beyond the grave?

But the second John, his father, is the subject of this chapter. The status of the three Johns – draper, surgeon, barrister–painter – tells its own story of 19th-century upward mobility. Of these three it was the middle one, John Forster, surgeon-to-be, who held the key to the family fortune. To find out how this happened we need to go back to the year 1821 and north to Northumberland: to another death, less dramatic than Gertrude's and with no contemporary account of it, but as important for the family as hers, if not more so.

So, to Alnwick, on an early January afternoon in 1821, to a sickroom where an elderly gentleman is breathing his last, attended by a young man in his 20s. Alnwick is a thriving market town, the agricultural centre of the county. It boasts a spectacular medieval castle, the home of the Dukes of Northumberland. Its cobbled streets are fronted by shops and imposing town housee. One of these, easily identified on that dark winter afternoon by the straw spread in the street outside, to muffle the clatter of wheels, is the home of the dying man.

He is William Baird, a wealthy landowner. And the young man with him, who is bringing all his professional skills to help the sick man in his extremity, is John Forster, surgeon, William Baird's favourite nephew.

William Baird's wealth derived from large estates about 50 miles north of Newcastle in and around the town of Alnwick and on the border. It was a good time to be a landowner. Agricultural incomes had soared during the Napoleonic wars, and in its aftermath wheat prices maintained three times their prewar level thanks to the notorious Corn Laws (not abolished till 1846) which protected the English corn producers' monopoly. In the 1820s the William Bairds of Britain were riding high.

John Forster, the draper, himself an Alnwick man, had married William Baird's sister Jane. They had eight children, four boys and four girls. With her connections and his trade, the Forsters must have been comfortably off. John Forster and his brother-in-law William Baird have matching monuments in Alnwick parish church, finely wrought slabs of marble commemorating these pillars of Northumbrian society, each wealthy in their own right. To judge by how much John-surgeon spent on drapery later (and this we know), it was a profitable field to be in. Again, there were spin-offs from the social upheavals wrought by the French wars. One has only to think of Jane Austen's nouveaux-riches characters, the Mr Bingleys and Admiral Crofts, eager to buy themselves into the landed gentry, to realize that anyone connected with the housing business, as drapers were, stood to gain. You just had to have a good head for business; and if John Forster father was anything like his son, he had.

John Forster, son, had been trained as a surgeon. Where he had done his apprenticeship we don't know – probably with a local surgeon. It was over 50 years since surgeons had separated themselves from barbers and formed their own company. The setting up of the Royal College of Surgeons in 1800 had given them new status (not high enough for some people: when Florence Nightingale was fighting one of her many battles with her family to be allowed to learn nursing her mother accused her of having a secret love affair with some 'low vulgar surgeon', and this was as late as 1845). But compared with the drapery business surgery was a definite step up. The young John Forster passed his qualifying exams for membership of the Royal College in London in 1812. Four years later he joined the team of surgeons at the Newcastle Infirmary, which had been rebuilt and enlarged at the turn of the century in response to the huge increase in the town's population over the previous 50 years.

What young John Forster did in the four years between qualifying and taking up his post at the Infirmary, we do not know. Maybe he was among the many surgeons who went abroad to join the support services of the army (at the time of the Battle of Waterloo in 1815 medical men flocked to the continent to help and, such were the relaxed rules of war, French and British surgeons would cross the lines to discuss interesting cases). More probably he stayed in the north, plying his trade as apothecary–surgeon. To judge by the equipment he bought when he set up shop in Newcastle after 1816 and ran a private practice alongside his job in the Infirmary, he was something of a jack of all surgical trades. Today's specialisms were unknown. He was obstetrician, eye-surgeon, orthopaedic surgeon – in fact prepared for any surgical eventuality

He faced quite an outlay on premises, furnishings and instruments. His father had died in 1812. Who was going to help? Enter Uncle William. '1816 May 12, Received of Mr Baird 1st £50; 2nd £20; 3rd £100; 4th £100; 5th £35', the young surgeon's account-book records. Together with consultation fees of a guinea a time and examinations ('5 men . . . 12/6') his income for the first five months of that year came to over £316. Not bad for a 19-year-old surgeon just set up in business, at a time when an industrial worker would be expected to survive on £70 a year and an office clerk on £90. To get the modern equivalent you have to multiply by a factor of more than 40 (the average for the whole century is nearer 50). So this represented about £13,000 in today's buying power, for not quite half a year. William Baird was very generous.

John Forster wrote it all down in a vellum-bound account book. Receipts at one end, expenditure at the other. Inside the front cover the life-and-death family events were noted with the time of day at which they happened, which is how we know that William Baird died at 3.30 pm on January 7th 1821 and 'My little Boy borne at 3 o'clock P.M.' on February 3rd 1823. The legacy gets no mention, but this was one thing he did not have to record. The whole account book is a monument to it.

Whoever was going to inherit the Baird fortune would be in for a lucky break. The young surgeon probably knew what was in store for him. The bonds that made him his uncle's favourite nephew (he was the third of the four sons) must have been forged over a long period.

The reading of the will took place in London on April 13th 1821. John Forster and his younger brother William, both major beneficiaries, were present. (John used the opportunity of the trip south to buy £8's worth of surgical instruments, a portmanteau, and two pairs of boots.) The will was a six-page document in seamless lawyer's-clerk script. Its length alone is evidence of the extent of the Baird estates. There are pages of detail about his properties ('messuages and herediments'), places with vivid names like Bloody Havers, Shoulder of Mutton Close and Windy Edge (we will come across this last again later). They were lived in by tenants whose interests had to be protected and their rents allocated among the legatees. William Baird left a clutch of annuities: £150 to his widowed sister Jane, John Forster's mother, £40 to Matthew her eldest son, £50 to Richard the second son; and lump sums of £1,000 each to her four daughters and his spinster sister-in-law, Frances Forster; then £25 went to each of his servants, £20 to the parish poor and so on. One senses the careful thought that lay behind each of these far-from-modest bequests. It is still the age of the extended family. With no children of his own William Baird made it his duty to provide for his wider family, particularly his widowed sister's.

The nub of the will comes after all these smaller bequests. The rest of the estate – probably about three-quarters of it – is to be divided between John and William Forster. William, the youngest nephew, gets the income from a long list of properties which on his death will go to his male descendants or failing that to his brother John and his male descendants; and John gets the income from an even longer list with the same proviso (that it goes to William if John dies without male issue, etc). The only catch was that they had to change their name to Baird, and adopt the Baird coat of arms. And anything left over, other monies that might materialize, should be invested in land.

Having burrowed one's way through the will, one reaches the end with a taste of earth in one's mouth. It is Northumbrian earth: the soil that William Baird grew rich on, the soil he wants to tether his heirs to. There were other areas to tempt investors then, with railways soon to be top of the list, but William Baird died too soon for railway-mania; anyway, land was what had made the family rich and land they should stick to. And the Baird name had to survive.

Changing your name to go with an inheritance was not unknown. Jane Austen's brother had done it, becoming Frank Knight of Godmersham Park; Florence Nightingale's father had been a William Shore till he came into a fortune left him by his uncle Peter Nightingale. One of the expenses listed in the account book of our John (now) Baird is the fee he paid for changing his name: £118 18s in June 1821. He also had to make three payments for legacy duty: two of £123 and one of £133. The metamorphosis in status did not come cheap.

One economy he made was not to apply to the College of Heralds for a new grant of arms. He adapted the Baird arms by adding Forster symbols, the bugles and the arm holding a spear that were emblems of that one-time clan of foresters. The Baird arms as they came down to us Baird descendants – on the remnants of family silver, odd spoons and forks – are a clever amalgam of the two coats of arms, Baird and Forster; but they are totally illegal in the strict heraldic sense. Either John Baird did not care enough to get them legalized or, more likely, he did not know he had to.

There is no way to quantify what his inheritance amounted to in total. But his meticulous accounts, which detail every item of receipt and expenditure, show a large income from rents, from commuted tithes and fees. For instance, between January and October 1821 he received £462; the following year £445, in 1824 £546, in 1827 £387, and so on. There are some mystery items: on September 25th 1818, he 'received £300', and five years later, in May 1823, there was £400 from a General Ker. These are huge sums of money. Were they gambling debts, or hush-money for advice on some dubious medical complaint? The army records show there were many Kers; they were a big family, also from the borders, but none with a known link with our surgeon.

The receipts suggest that John Baird had more than enough money not to have to work. But he did. He was certainly a liberal spender, and it builds up as he gets established in his career. He moved house several times and acquired 'some notoriety', according to a history of Newcastle Infirmary, for building two stone houses, as opposed to the traditional brick, in Northumberland Street. Today Northumberland Street is one of the town's main arteries, a pedestrianized line of chain stores with nary a stone house in sight. I take it as evidence of John Baird's business acumen – one house to live in and perhaps one to rent – and stone seems a sensible building material for that part of the world.

The first page in his account book records relatively modest outgoings: two loads of potatoes for 1/4d, surgical instruments for £10 19s, eye instruments for £2 19s, a carriage 2/4d (hire for the month?), coals, table linen, blankets. He is setting up surgery and house. And so on it goes, month after month, year after year. He installed gas pipes for lighting in 1819, bought a backgammon board, a dog – a pointer – to go with the shooting he enjoyed on the Northumbrian moors, horses, books (over £30 on a collection that included Euclid, Burke's *On the Sublime*, and four novels by Sir Walter Scott) and more surgical instruments; all this in addition to paying builders, architects, painters, saddlers, carriage-makers, chemists (he buys a lot of drugs) and drapers, this last rarely less than £50 a year, often nearer £100. And he got the family portraits painted.

Without these portraits this chapter would have been almost impossible to write. But these watercolours show a man, his wife and four children with a subtle quality of painting that gives them an almost breathing presence. These are people whose handshake you can imagine – the firm father's, the hesitant wife's, the shy elder children's, the chubby baby's clenched fist.

29

The artist was a local man, Edward Hastings, well known in the north of the country. The first two portraits, of John Baird and his wife, were painted in 1827 for the cost of 7 guineas. John Baird is shown as a slight, curly-haired young man with serious, compassionate eyes. The artist has caught a very human face and a youthful one, in spite of the hint of a worry line above his right eye. It was quite a shock to find this picture reproduced in the history of the Infirmary alongside pictures of John Baird's colleagues, grizzled dignitaries looking twice his age. Perhaps it was his youthful charm which made him, like the biblical Joseph, loved above all his siblings by his uncle. We have to imagine him speaking with a Northumbrian accent, the strongly-consonanted lilt of the region.

He had married in the summer after Uncle William's death. His wife was Mary Potts – 'the beautiful Miss Potts', my grandmother (her granddaughter) always called her, as if that was how she had been christened. Mary Potts' father lived in a Newcastle property in Pandon Bank, near a park at the top of the town. Presumably the marriage was a love-match and, given John Baird's circumstances, probably one that made both families happy. John and Mary Baird had four children in the first five years of their marriage: John Forster, Mary Lowes, Jane Frances and Anna Maria; then another boy, William, born after a long gap in 1836. (John Baird surely participated in his wife's confinements: midwifery equipment – forceps – had been one of his early purchases.) That family-record page in the account book tells a moving story. The second daughter's entry reads: 'July 28th 1824 My little Girl borne at ½ past 9 o'clock P.M. Mary Lowes Baird [the next sentence is in a different shade of ink] Departed this life August 21st 1831 at 5 o'clock a.m'. The 1831 bereavement was probably the reason why no more children were born for another five years.

Mary Potts has a rather hesitant beauty under her muslin bonnet; appealing wide-spaced blue eyes and an attractive mouth. This is all we know of her. With her younger daughter, Anna Maria, her history must remain a blank. By contrast, the rest of the family are old familiars. There is John Forster Baird, then a shrinking 14-year-old, trussed up and ready for his new school: he is shortly off to Rugby (these pictures of the children were painted ten years after the first lot). Then Jane, with her head fetchingly tilted on one side, the future Auntie Jane whom we have already met. She lived with my grandmother's family in old age and died in 1912, when my mother was 16. 'Her feet died before the rest of her', was the story I heard as a child, which appalled and fascinated me in equal measure. (Poor Auntie Jane, I think now – and poor them nursing her at home with her gangrenous feet.) The next portrait is Anna Maria's, every flaxen doll-like inch of her the little sister. Finally there is William, a unisex baby dressed in girl's clothes, aged about a year. He, William, became a clergyman and made a 'disastrous marriage' according to my grandmother. But like Auntie Jane's feet, these were shadows undreamt of when the Baird children sat for those delicate portraits in 1837.

These pictures have their own story. After John Forster Baird's death my grandmother inherited them. When many years later, as wife of the Master of Balliol she entertained Queen Mary, wife of George V, on the occasion of a royal visit to Oxford after the First World War, she found the Queen eyeing the pictures with beady interest. 'They would look very nice in Windsor,' said Her Majesty. 'Not as nice as they look here, ma'am,' was my grandmother's firm reply. So in the family they stayed, like household gods, to be handed down the generations.

The painting of his family by a leading local artist marked John Baird's growing status as an established professional man.

His name began to appear in print. He was involved in the setting up of the Newcastle medical school in 1834, the 'eminent surgeon' whose lectures for students (two guineas for a six-month course) were billed in the local press. There was again shortage of space in the hospital. Professional jealousy and hostility to innovation among the older staff made life difficult for the founders of the new school. Another problem was public outrage at the idea of dissection. Altogether it cannot have been easy for the young teaching team. I have asked myself whether John Baird's windfall inheritance dented his commitment to his work and have come to the conclusion it did not. Rather the reverse. He almost certainly subsidized his career out of his private income – all those expensive surgical instruments, for instance. Not all his patients would have been able to pay a fat fee.

At about this time he was appointed senior surgeon at the Infirmary. It was in that capacity that he took part in the annual meeting of the British Association, in November 1838, described in a contemporary journal as a week of important scientific business 'unparalleled of its kind'. The British Association for the Advancement of Science had been founded five years earlier, after Charles Babbage had written an article criticizing the decline of science in England and the lack of leadership provided by the Royal Society. The association saw itself as in the forefront of science and technology, committed to providing a forum for scientific talent, amateur as well as professional, throughout the country. Babbage himself, designer of the first mechanical calculator and at that time working on the analytical engine, a programmable calculating machine, was at the Newcastle meeting; other luminaries included Sir John Herschel, the mathematician and astronomer, who read a paper on Halley's Comet, and Kershaw, the optics expert. Over 200 papers were read to sessions divided into seven disciplines: mathematics, chemistry, geology, mechanics, zoology, statistics and medicine. Under this last category John Baird presented his paper, the only surgical one: 'On a Successful Excision of the Elbow Joint' (an operation perhaps performed after an industrial accident).

Before the meeting John Baird had written to Thomas Arnold, headmaster of Rugby where his son had been for just over a year, inviting him to the Newcastle proceedings. It would be a good moment to meet the famous teacher (if he had not already) and impress him with the vitality and excitement of the scientific world he himself felt part of. We do not have John Baird's letter, but Dr Arnold's reply has survived. It is a polite refusal. Regretfully, the great headmaster says, he does not have the time, besides which 'I am so little of a scientific Man that I have always felt that I should be out of Place at such a meeting.' What, one wonders, would it have meant for the future of English education if he had accepted with delight and said that science was what interested him above all else? The classical bias of the Rugby model was to stamp it for the next 100 years.

The organization Dr Arnold turned his back on was self-consciously innovative. Reading the association's programme one senses its almost missionary zeal. Darwin's *Origin of Species* was still 20 years ahead, as was – more to the point for John Baird – the first use of anaesthesia by injection, but the ground was being prepared for these and other earth-shaking advances by those gentlemen in Newcastle, and others like them, with their passionate involvement in their chosen specialisms. It was furthermore a matter of pride for the association that women were admitted to some of the meetings. Women's interest in things scientific, reported the secretary, was the main reason for 'the diffusion of taste for science among the rising generation'.

The ladies could only be present, though, if the subject were suitable. There was a paper presented by a Dr Adams on 'The Placental Soufflé' which I imagine they were barred from, as they were no doubt from John Baird's paper with its details of pre-anaesthesia surgery.

Surgery in those days was a grisly trade. The first operation using anaesthesia did not take place till 1846; its use would not become popular till Queen Victoria allowed Dr John Snow, later famous for his work on cholera and also a one-time student at the Newcastle medical school, to administer 'that blessed chloroform' when she was in labour with Prince Leopold in 1853.

All this was after John Baird's time. We have only to look at his expenditure on wines and spirits to see what was the only form of anaesthesia available in pre-chloroform days. Patients would be rendered as far as possible insensible with drink. The alternative was to tie them down. A contemporary described patients awaiting operations like criminals preparing for execution, and all but the most hardened surgeons shared this dread. John Keats, who qualified in London a few years after John Baird, practised for a short time and then gave it up not just because he wanted to write poetry but because he was terrified at the damage he might inadvertently do: 'My last operation was the opening of a man's temporal artery,' his friend Charles Brown reported him as saying. 'I did it with the utmost nicety; but, reflecting on what passed through my mind at the time, my dexterity seemed a miracle, and I never took up the lancet again.' Laurence Irving, John Baird's great-grandson (and the son of Dolly, the two-year-old who threw flowers into Gertrude's grave) gave a lurid description of John Baird's work in his book *The Successors*: 'He continued in practice . . . probably in a frock coat kept for the purpose, stained with blood and pus and host to septic agents too often claiming the life that his surgery had saved. Sometimes after major operations he was himself in a state of collapse.' And, as we shall see, there were other infectious agents around waiting to attack doctor as well as patient.

One surgical event John Baird had taken part in a few years earlier that had none of the usual terrors of the knife was the 'opening' of an Egyptian mummy, this at the invitation of the Newcastle Literary and Philosophical Society. Baird was a member of the society. He and a fellow surgeon from the Infirmary were invited to do a demonstration dissection, spanning two successive evenings. The mummy had been donated by a Mr Wright who had purchased it during his travels in Egypt. Wright had also met M. Champollion, later famous for deciphering the Rosetta Stone, and the latter had translated the hieroglyphs on the mummy case for him.

One can imagine the scene: the mummy in its case on the table, the excitement of the audience as the musty wrappings were removed and the desiccated remains revealed. For the surgeons it was a great opportunity. Cadavers were still expensive; the days of body-snatchers and churchyard guardhouses were very recent. It would be a relief too to be able to practise surgical skills on a body several millennia beyond the reach of pain.

In 1843 John Baird reached the peak of his career when he was made Fellow of the Royal College of Surgeons, one of the 300 founding Fellows. (There were three prerequisites for this: 20 years of college membership, a consistent record of eminence as a surgeon and the recommendation of another fellow, in this case unknown.) His social status meanwhile mirrored his professional success. The family had moved to Charlotte Square, a late Georgian garden square in the centre of Newcastle; and, as the census of 1841 (the first in the north) shows us, he had a well-appointed household.

It consisted of himself, John Baird, aged 45; his wife Mary, aged 40; the 30-year-old Frances Potts whom we have met in the later Teddington census, and William, the youngest child who is four. There is no sign of the daughters; perhaps they were being educated by an aunt or grandmother away from home. John, the eldest, was at Rugby.

The rest of the household are servants and one lodger, Charles Martin, a surgical apprentice who would have paid between £100 and £150 in annual apprenticeship fees. There is a manservant, Thomas McGuire, and three maids, Alice Johnson, 35, Jean Cumming, 25, and Isabella Codling, 30. Alice Johnson was a local girl like the others, but she had a special relationship with her employers and we shall meet her again. Together with the family they comprise a compact household, the comfortable menage of the successful professional man. Elsewhere, though, there are signs that all is not well.

Our other source, the account book, tells a different story. The entries are becoming more rapid, the writing wilder. Here is a man in a hurry to fit everything in. It is as if he suddenly realizes that time is running out.

How much did he know, or guess, about his own state of health? Tuberculosis can throw a long shadow before it. But even an experienced surgeon may ignore symptoms or if he diagnoses them can decide the best thing to do is nothing. In those days there was little choice. Thousands of people in Britain were doing just that, living with symptoms they could do nothing about. On April 5th 1844 John Baird began closing down his Newcastle life. He made his last entry in his account book: 'Sent the closed carriage to Mrs Burroughs. All the horses & Pony put off work, and not to be used again, but to be sent out to the grass as soon as there is grass for them.' He then paid some outstanding bills – the draper's, the cutler's the saddler's – and headed south for London by sea.

There is a state of mind known as *spes phthisica*, the consumptive's (false) hope, a conviction of recovery which can come upon the patient in the penultimate phase of the illness. Is this what made John Baird leave Newcastle, a belief that after a sea journey and in the milder climate of London his health would improve? He took with him the maidservant Alice Johnson. She would have been 38 in 1844, John Baird ten years older. Was this a romance, I wondered conventionally, when I saw her name on his death certificate as the person who had been with him when he died? But when I next came across Alice's name it was on the death certificate, 12 years later, of Mary Baird, John's wife, who also died of tuberculosis. Alice was the loyal family servant who stayed with her employers to the end.

I wondered whether Mary Baird had been one of the London party, then decided she would have stayed at home with William, who was then seven. We will never know if John left her with the assurance that he would soon be back, cured, or they both knew it was the end. Possibly he went south to see some specialist-colleague who had a reputation for working miracle cures, although miracle cures for tuberculosis, society's top killer, did not exist. It was common for people to seek the warm south; Chopin went to Majorca, Keats to Rome. We meet another of the 'white plague's' victims later, in Mary's diary, a Charles Griffith (with whom she becomes enamoured) who is doing just the same, desperately going south in search of health. John Baird was only doing what countless others had done before and would do after him.

He took rooms at 1 Addison Terrace, Kensington. It was there he spent his last weeks. John Forster Baird, then at university, visited his dying father. There is an undated sketch of his of the street view from a first-floor window, presumably his father's room. On June 5th John Baird summoned lawyers and made his will. (The fact that he had not made one before substantiates the idea that he did not know, or did not believe, that he was terminally ill until the very end.) In contrast to his uncle's, which had begun his ascent in the world, this was a very modest document. Two pages, with the lines well-spaced and the writing amazingly legible; a simpler document dictated in the room where the sick man lay. He died ten days later, on June 15th 1844. A notice of his death appeared later that week in the *Newcastle Courant*: 'At London, on the 15 inst, deeply and most deservedly lamented, John Baird Esq., an eminent surgeon of this town; whose private worth and professional skill will cause his loss to be greatly felt.'

The disposition of his assets was very simple. Two debts to his son ('my dear son John Forster Baird') arising from the purchase of a Northumberland property and totalling just over £2,000 were to be repaid out of the estate. All the rest was to go to his wife and after her death to the other three younger children, 'my dear eldest son being fully provided for'. The will concluded with the stock phrase: 'Effects sworn under [in this case] £7,000' (about £350,000 in modern terms). This of course was in addition to whatever he had settled on his eldest son. In what way John Forster Baird had been provided for we only know in outline. He had been sent away to school, one of the best in the country, and from there he had gone on to university.

The story of his education will be told in the next chapter, but there is a coda to this one. A cousin and I went to look for John Baird's grave. He had died in London, so it should be easy to find. A helpful librarian at the Kensington local history library pointed the way to the Brompton cemetery. Yes, the Baird name was on their list, two Bairds, in fact: William was buried in the same grave as his father. (He too died of tuberculosis, 31 years later; it was because of his death that Mary was wearing mourning on that sweltering Boat Race Saturday in 1876.)

Following the grid plan, we found the plot: but there was no gravestone. Both deaths had gone unmarked. And as I stared at the scrubby rectangle of grass, a picture began to form: of Mary Baird, widow, stuck in Newcastle, leaving details like the question of a gravestone to her educated elder son with his knowledge of southern ways; of John Forster Baird, just finishing his university degree and about to take off on his Grand Tour. The gravestone had simply been forgotten. Thirty-odd years later there was another funeral in the same cemetery: but then, four months after William's death, Gertrude's death shattered the family and put all thoughts of any other gravestone out of her father's mind.

3   *School for Christian Gentlemen*

A Temple of industrious peace.
Thomas Carlyle, describing Rugby, 1842

He harangued his pupils from the pulpit, he was a firm believer in corporal punishment and he said he would rather have his son believe the sun went round the earth than 'have physical science the principal thing in his mind'. Yet Thomas Arnold – this lion of a man – was also revered by the boys, and he used some of the most enlightened teaching methods of his age.

In choosing Rugby for his son John Baird had gone for the best (at £110 a year, which he could well afford). Dr Arnold had been appointed headmaster in 1829. By the time John Forster Baird arrived there in 1837 the school's reputation as the training ground for an educated elite was firmly established. But it was not an academic elite. Arnold's primary aim was to produce Christian gentlemen: 'What we must look for here is, first, religious and moral principle; secondly, gentlemanly conduct; thirdly, intellectual ability' – such was his order of priorities. In *Tom Brown's Schooldays* by the ex-Rugbeian Thomas Hughes, Tom's father, Squire Brown, puts the same thought more directly: 'I don't care a straw for Greek particles. . . . If he only turns out a brave, helpful, truth telling Englishman, and a gentleman, and a Christian, that's all I want.'

The demand for such educated (Christian) gentlemen was growing. As government business expanded, a more versatile bureaucracy was required. The educated middle classes could fill this need, people like Thomas Arnold's eldest son, the poet Matthew, John Forster Baird's near contemporary, who was to build a career as inspector of education. He, Matthew, was sardonic about the 'grand old, fortifying, classical curriculum' offered in his father's school. But classics was not just a linguistic discipline. It provided a model for empire-building. Part of Thomas Arnold's success was due to timing. His principled education arrived in a world increasingly dominated by *pax britannica*, whether in the form of missionaries or railways. The top industrial nation needed an ideological rationale for its vision of world rule. Arnold's high morality – his temple of industrious peace – fitted well into the scheme of things.

The Arnold system included an innovatory approach that was not immediately apparent from the timetable. Between three and four hours' classics every morning (and two to three hours' classics homework), four hours a week for mathematics, two for modern history, English literature and foreign languages (introduced later) – nothing was very new here. But it was Arnold's personal method that was unusual. His aim, said one ex-pupil, was 'not so much to impart information as to awaken thought. . . . Instead of giving the explanation at once he would place himself, so to speak, at the side of his pupils and help them find it for themselves.' How his pupils learnt was as important to him as what they learnt. This shift in emphasis from content to process is still controversial 170 years later, and was typical of a man who often sided with causes that went against the mood of the times. He had spoken out for religious tolerance against the extremists in the Oxford movement ('Oxford malignants', as he called them) which provoked his school governors into trying to have him suspended. But the man who had trebled the school's intake was not so easily dislodged. For every enemy he made, he had twice as many devotees.

Was John Forster Baird one of them? The young Newcastle lad was 14 when he arrived. We have that picture of him looking frightened before he had even left home; and we can only imagine what went through his mind when he saw those huge grounds, that high castellated main building, and the awesome chapel.

Baird (as he would have been known) went into the Fifth Form, which was lucky; he was too old to be a fag, and so would not run the risk of being roasted in front of the prefects' fire, like poor Tom Brown. But how happy was he, how well did he adapt to this new world of shared dormitories, 5 a.m. starts and an almost undiluted diet of classics and Christianity? He went into the house of one of the staff, the Reverend Buckoll, a famous preacher; but whether the Reverend was a good teacher as well, we don't know. Young Baird performed fairly abysmally in his first end-of-year exams, coming third from the bottom (64th out of 69) that first December. The following summer, still in the Lower Fifth, he did better (19th out of 50); six months later, at Christmas 1838, he was half-way down the Middle Fifth Form list.

One cannot necessarily read homesickness into these results. But it would have been strange if he had not missed home, and one wonders how much the boy with the easily mimicked north-country accent was teased (and how soon he managed to iron it out). At the beginning of his second year at school he received a letter from an aunt, Anne Potts, writing from Hull, in which she says she is glad to hear that he is happy, not a fag ('I certainly have no good impression of the fagging system'), and getting on so well with his studies. 'Many advantages you have of meeting the brightest hopes of your friends,' she writes. There is a sense of a family investing everything in this eldest son, of expectations of the glory he will bring – heavy stuff for a 15-year-old, but normal in those days, particularly where a step up the class ladder was involved. But why the letter survived, I suspect, is because of the momentous local news it contained. This is September 1838; there have been exceptional equinoctial gales in the North Sea.

You have perhaps heard of the dreadful shipwreck of one of the Hull steam packets [S.S. *Forfarshire*] on the [Farne] island; above 40 individuals have lost their lives, and only eighteen saved nine of whom were rescued from the wreck by Mr Darling (who keeps the lighthouse) and his daughter who greatly risked their own lives to save the lives of these poor creatures. I feel proud indeed of my *county woman*, but I intend to send you a Hull newspaper with particulars as I am sure you will feel greatly interested as you so well know the place.

Anne Potts was clearly thrilled by the bravery of Grace Darling, as a woman and fellow Northumbrian. She then handed her letter to be finished by the friend she was staying with, a Mrs Newmarsh, who was John's godmother. Mrs Newmarsh brings us back to more sober realities. 'I still feel great interest in the dear boy for whom I promised at his baptism,' she wrote. 'Soon you will take these promises on yourself and I wish you well to consider the vast importance of them. You are now placed in a situation of many temptations, but from the good accounts I hear of you I believe the Grace of God had hitherto kept you from great sins and ever remember dear John you cannot in your own strength do anything pleasing to God and after all however you may shine in the world as a man of science or of letters you will fall very short if you do not make the Saviour of God your first consideration and try to glorify him in all things.'

The new morality was being preached on all sides. I doubt if

Dr Arnold and Mrs Newmarsh ever met, but they would have surely got on if they had. At about that time Arnold had preached one of his thunderous school sermons: 'How is it with you now? . . . Do you think of God *now*? . . . Do you say your prayers to him? . . . Do you still love to be kind to your companions, never teasing or ill-treating them? . . . Are you still anxious to please your parents?' John Forster Baird could probably answer yes to all these questions. But what that really meant was another matter. His diaries are not those of a particularly religious man. Surprisingly little of what was known as the 'Rugby earnestness' seems to have rubbed off on him. All in all, by the time he left he had acquired the outward veneer of the southern public-school man, its affability (except when very ruffled) and social ease, but he had been too long imprinted with the north and with his family (his father's outdoor interests, his own love of the border country) not to feel, underneath, that that was where he really belonged.

The school offered drawing as an optional extra. The drawing master was a local artist, Edward Rudge, who taught there from 1824 to 1841. Rudge specialized in watercolour landscapes; one of his pictures, a village scene, was exhibited at the Royal Academy. We have no means of knowing whether John Forster Baird attended his classes, but it is inconceivable to me that he would not have drawing lessons when they were on offer at school, given his later commitment to his art. The inner potential of each pupil was, after all, something the Arnold system aimed to develop. This could well have been the point where John Forster Baird decided to take his love of painting seriously.

There was another Rugby boy, at the same time, who was quietly developing his creative talent alongside the daily school routine. Both of these young men would live dual lives – an outer professional one and an inner creative one – when they went on into adult life. But there the parallel stops. Matthew Arnold, Dr Arnold's eldest son, was two months older than John Forster Baird (born in December 1822 to John Forster Baird's February 1823). Matthew had gone into his father's house, School House, where John Forster Baird only went in his last year, after Matthew had left. They would have met, though, in the Sixth Form. The Sixth consisted of about 16 praepostors (prefects) and a group called the Twenty, Arnold's elite pupils whom he regarded as a cross between favourite nephews and apostles; when he lost the confidence of his Sixth, he said, he would know it was time to retire. John Forster Baird appears briefly among the Twenty in June 1840, then his name disappears. Six months later he is a simple member of the Upper School (was this a demotion?), but a year later he is back, this time as a praepostor, and he remained a prefect until he left, in the spring of 1842. During that summer of 1840, when John Forster Baird was in the Twenty, Matthew Arnold was a praepostor. Did the two ever strike up more than a casual acquaintanceship, one wonders? They would have had a lot in common, if they had ever got beyond the outer layers of friendship. But in fact the later differences between them were as great as the early similarities. Matthew Arnold was *par excellence* a member of the establishment, his successful career, as poet as well as a remarkable schools' inspector, vouchsafed by both parentage and education as well as talent.

Matthew was to win the coveted Balliol scholarship, regarded as the crowning glory of a Rugby career, notwithstanding the lowly emphasis placed on intellectual prowess. Would it be possible, John Baird had asked in his 1838 letter to Dr Arnold inviting him to the British Association meeting, for his own son's name to be put forward for the Balliol scholarship? Arnold first dealt with the matter of the invitation (as we have seen), then turned to the question of his pupil's academic prospects. His letter is a model of how to deliver uncomfortable news to an aspiring parent tactfully.

Your son is quite well and getting on well, I think, in his Form. . . . I would myself have applied to the Master of Balliol on his behalf, but I have made it an Invariable Rule never to apply for any Boy at this school except on public Grounds – that is, when a Boy is doing so well that I can really recommend him for admission at a good College, *Honoris causa* [by reason of merit]. Even this however would be useless at Balliol, for the Master told me some Time since that he was engaged for so long a Period that he did not like to enter any new Names on his List; this was his Answer when I applied to him in Behalf of my own eldest son.

Arnold's erratic use of capitals betrays his unease. His letter in fact told less than the truth. For the headmaster's son only the best would do: Matthew was soon to be coached for the Balliol scholarship (which he would win).

The Bairds would get their own back later, when John Forster Baird's eldest daughter married a future Master of Balliol who would one day tutor Thomas Arnold's great-grandson. But for the time being, the gates of Balliol were closed. John Forster Baird had to turn elsewhere. His choice was Cambridge, and in May 1842 he went up to Trinity College.

Byron had found it a dismal place. Darwin, advising his son not to go there, said there would be too much temptation to be idle at Trinity ('it is hard enough for the young to be industrious'). In the mid-19th century Cambridge had a reputation for serious socializing and equally serious academic competitiveness – in either case, 24 weeks of intense living every year for three or four years. John Forster Baird's record, however, suggests he was neither excessively industrious nor an out-and-out socialite. His father's death, occurring in the middle of his time there, must have coloured his whole Cambridge experience; and, as we have seen from the evidence of his sketch of Addison Road, he left during his second summer term to be with his dying father in London.

He read for an honours degree, and had recovered from the family tragedy sufficiently to rank third among the Senior Optimes in the summer 1846 Tripos List. Honours degrees were grouped into three classes: Wranglers (the equivalent of today's Firsts), Senior Optimes (Seconds) and Junior Optimes (Thirds and Fourths); thus his result was the equivalent of a top 2:1 today. His subject was maths, probably laced with classics. (The supremacy of mathematics at Cambridge, Newton's legacy, made the Maths Tripos compulsory in the 19th century; the Classical Tripos was voluntary and there was no Law Tripos till 1858, so even if John Forster Baird already intended to study law he could have done nothing about it.) His father's illness and death might, strangely, have helped him to concentrate on his work: at such a time study can become an emotional anchor. Whatever the reasons, his creditable result in the final exams must have entailed quite a lot of hard work. The one surviving letter of his from this period, to his mother in March 1844, ends: 'As I have about twenty pages of Differential Calculus to read tonight for an examination tomorrow I must say goodnight, with love to Papa, Jane, William and yourself.' There is no mention of sister Anna, but a revealing reference to his father's health: 'I was glad to hear from your last letter that Papa had hopes of getting out, but I think if the weather continues as raw and cold as it has hitherto done the longer he stays in the better.' (This was three months before his father's death.)

John Forster Baird had joined the Cambridge Union, the debating society, soon after he went to Trinity; and, except when he was briefly banned in the spring of 1845 for non-payment of fines and arrears, he remained a member throughout his time at Cambridge. Trinity men tended to dominate the Union debates; John Forster Baird attended as a non-contributory member (i.e. not speaking in any of the debates). But in the spring of 1846 he was elected Union president, a position he held for a month. There were some interesting debates during that month; only the briefest of minuted records survive, but the voting pattern is indicative.

The first debate during John Forster Baird's tenure was on the motion, 'That the introduction of the New Poor Law has been beneficial to this Country'. This touched on an issue that was provoking burning resentment among the working classes. Under the 1834 Poor Law Amendment Act, in lieu of local poor rates (the Speenhamland system), a centralized system had been set up whose main pillar was the workhouse. Paupers, as the poor of all ages were called, would have their relief stopped and instead be sent to workhouses, men to one house, women to another. The problem of poverty would thus be tidied away. The appointment of Poor Law Commissioners and later a Poor Law Board created a pyramid of machinery to administer the act. Meanwhile, what went on behind the doors of the workhouse was not the concern of those who championed this neat solution to one of the crueller problems of the age.

The Union debaters voted enthusiastically for the motion and in favour of the new law – 24 for and 11 against. (Dr Arnold, who had encouraged his pupils to visit the poor with him, had concentrated on the 'good poor'.) The next debate, a week later, was on the motion, 'That our present system of Transportation is fraught with much evil', and this time it was lost, ayes 10 and noes 54. The young gentlemen of Cambridge slept more comfortably in their beds with the thought of convicted criminals – machine-breakers and rick-burners, pickpockets and burglars – being packed off to the antipodes. Three weeks later (after two sessions debating whether 'Her Majesty's Ministers are unworthy of the confidence of the Country') came a debate on a motion that must have interested John Forster Baird and any other landowning young men there, 'That the agitation carried on by the Anti-Corn-Law League has been both illegal and unconstitutional'.

The Corn Laws had kept bread prices artificially high since 1815, much to the benefit of cereal-producing landlords and ultimately of the rural lobby, though there were complaints at the high wages agricultural workers demanded when the price of bread rose. Six months before this debate in the Cambridge Union the failure of the Irish potato crop, coupled with deluging rain in England which had wrecked the wheat crop, led to famine in Ireland and widespread agitation on the mainland. The manufacturing community meanwhile was against the Corn Laws since import controls undermined their exports. It was an issue which affected nearly every aspect of the economy as well as one that raised moral and political questions (when Sir Robert Peel finally repealed the Corn Laws, he split his party). Our Cambridge group, expectedly, remained true to their colours. The motion was carried: ayes 42, noes 13. The last debate of John Forster Baird's tenure as president focused on what many people believed was the root of all evil, the 1832 Parliamentary Reform Bill. The motion, 'That the circumstances of the present age tend amply to prove the great evils of the Democratic Principles embodied in the Reform Bill', was passed by 25 to 17; but at least well over a third of those present voted for this reluctant step towards democracy.

What we do not know is what side the president was on. As chairman he was silent in the debate. It is a fair guess that he sided with the conservative majority. These issues, which were tearing England apart and making the 1840s one of the most turbulent decades in the 19th century, did not deeply dent the lives of people like him or his fellow students. From the distance of today the two Englands of those times (Disraeli's 'inhabitants of different planets . . . the Rich and the Poor') seem like two continents separated by an uncrossable chasm. The rare spirits who did span them or took action to ameliorate things, and the literature that grew out of their awareness, help our retrospective understanding; but they probably made as little impact on the more prosperous members of society then as accounts of the child poverty that still exists do today, over a century and a half later. My point is that we must not be too harsh on the John Forster Bairds. Their limitations foreshadow our own.

This is a very skeletal account of my great-grandfather's Cambridge days. He filled three years of life there and we only have fragments of information about it. He remains an elusive character, like a figure in an ancient etching of King's Parade, gowned and sleek-trousered: the gentleman undergraduate. What other things he did – drama, sport or art – we do not know. After his June exams in 1846 for the first time in a decade or longer he was free of formal education. The forests of south Germany beckoned, and beyond them, Italy; and now he started to keep a journal.

4   *The Grand Tour*

The whole scene had an exquisitely foreign appearance.
John Forster Baird, on the Grand Place, Brussels,
June 1846

John Forster Baird's first two continental trips, from June to August 1846 and July to August 1847, were the formative experiences of his life. They gave him a passion for travel which never left him. The freedom of life in a foreign culture where one could shake off home responsibilities, the awesome beauty of the Alps, the physical joy of exploring mountain tracks always sure of a good meal and safe lodging at the end of the day – this was the Europe he experienced during those five months of travel.

There was another world he did not see, the Europe of bursting towns and radical ferment. In 1847 Marx and Engels were working on a draft of the Communist Manifesto, which would be published a year later. Bad harvests in the summer of 1847 combined with a business slump to create unprecedented discontent in the towns, and growing nationalism would erupt a year later in revolutions that swept the continent. But like all British travellers – those on the invalid trail, or artists and writers like Dickens, Trollope or Ruskin who sought the stimulus and exoticism of foreign parts – John Forster Baird was looking for what was different, not what was the same. Each of these people found it in their own way. His way was to seek out the heart of a place with his eye, then capture it on paper with his brush.

The portfolios of his journeys are both photograph albums, a visual record of his travels, and much more. They accompany the journals that were written for his mother and family. The journals have a slightly stilted quality, as censored reportage for the folks at home can have, particularly when one is young. But reading his text, looking at these pictures and sketchbooks which always went with him, you begin to feel that love of abroad was something he absorbed by a kind of osmosis. Each sketch he did made it more a part of his being; and having been absorbed it was lodged in him for life.

He was already signed up for the Bar. Most probably that had been part of the provision made for him which John Baird had referred to in his will. If his father had willed it, there was no way he could do other than obey. Besides, a gentleman had to find some professional niche, some alternative source of income against a rainy day (particularly necessary given the recent fluctuations in agricultural incomes after the happy plateau of the last two decades). The Bar therefore might appear an attractive option.

Yet, yet. . . . Since the 1830s and earlier Newcastle had been home to a school of artists, watercolourists who had built up a fine reputation, people like Thomas Miles Richardson, John Wilson Carmichael, James Ramsay and John Dobson, the two last painting in an architectural style – which makes me wonder whether the 15 guineas that John Baird paid to a Mr Dobson, architect, in 1831 was for drawing lessons for his son. Be that as it may, there is no doubt John Forster Baird was exposed to the work of these artists: an entry in his journal refers to Richardson's son who was also an artist, and who appears to have been a friend of his. Growing up among these people, he must have realized it was possible to secure an honourable place in society by art alone. In the end, his adult life was split. He became, in public, the 'barrister at law' of the later census; in private he was the nomadic artist who dragged his family round Europe at his genie's command.

His first taste of it, the first whiff of delights to come, was recorded in his 1846 journal: and strangely it was England that gave him this sense of novelty, a part of the country as unfamiliar to him as abroad, the Medway valley. He chose a roundabout route to the Ramsgate boat which was going to take him across to Ostend. 'The view of the road from Chatham to Canterbury well repaid me for any additional trouble which I experienced from adopting such a circuitous route.' That broad wooded valley curving down to the river, with the castle and cathedral of Rochester guarding its southern flank – he viewed it all with contented, happy appreciation; and this is his tone throughout the diary. Even Ostend, which had 'nothing very remarkable about it', did not strike him as being 'such a dirty place as all travellers and guide books would fain have us believe'. It was Brussels, the Hôtel de Ville and market in the square in front of it, which evoked his first superlatives. The evening was spent absorbing its exquisite foreignness, watching the carriages and strollers in the boulevards, the crowds in the open-air cafés. Abroad had begun.

The journal is 192 pages long and divided into chapters. The first ends at the Belgian–Prussian border; Chapter 2 takes us down the Rhine by boat, Chapter 3 across to Heidelberg and Freiburg by train, Chapter 4 to Switzerland by 'voiture' through the Black Forest and Swiss Alps. Switzerland takes up three chapters, Italy six. The last five chapters, when he took the homeward route through the Tyrol to Vienna and Prague and north, included in the contents page at the beginning, are missing, possibly never written.

He broke his journey along the route, stopping for several days in different places – Freiburg, for instance. His account of his stay there is typical of his wide-eyed wonder. It was, he wrote, one of the prettiest towns he had seen in Germany ('the cathedral is second only to that of Strasbourg, and if anything rather superior to it in the richness of its tracery . . . the spire is formed with the most exquisite open tracery'). Later that day he was given a booklet about the cathedral by its author, the commissionaire of the hotel where he was staying, the Zahringer Hof, who guided him round the city. He then walked out of town and up the Schönberg to see the view across to the distant Rhine, and after 'an excellent table d'hôte' went to a concert (conducted by Herr J. Hein, 'a young man of great musical power'). He could not understand, he says, why *Murray's Guide*, which he had with him, gave the Zahringer Hof bad marks. He left Freiburg the next morning, but was too late for the 4 a.m. diligence so hired a chaise ('we' hired a chaise, he says) and caught up with it before it reached the end of its first stage.

He was not travelling alone. No name is mentioned, and mostly the journal describes what 'I' did. But there is a shadowy companion, possibly Newman Hall, the friend who was to accompany him on the following year's trip. What we know about the Freiburg visit which he doesn't tell us is that he sketched the city. A drawing of it has survived, and is now hanging, appropriately, in the city where it was done, though the vineyards where the view of the cathedral (*Münster*) was drawn have since been gobbled up by buildings. It shows a village-sized town clustered round its cathedral with a border of meadows stretching up to the mountains of the Schwarzwald. (The railway that had brought him there was soon to change all that.)

Germany and Italy at that time were a patchwork of principalities and borders. Bismarck (eight years older than John Forster Baird) may have been dreaming of German unification under Prussia, and across the Alps Cavour and Mazzini were agitating for a united Italy free of foreign domination, but it would be another 20 years before that happened and in the meantime Europe was still the hotchpotch it had been left in the wake of the Napoleonic wars. For travellers this meant endless customs checks as they crossed from state to state. At the top of each page John Forster Baird noted what country/ principality he was in: Belgium first; then just before Aix la Chapelle (Aachen) he crossed into Prussia (passport check), then into the duchy of Nassau as he went up the Rhine, and after Mainz into Baden which stretched south to Switzerland. Italy (Savoy) started after the Simplon pass but it was under the rule of the kingdom of Sardinia; then at Seste Calende where Lombardy began the luggage was opened by 'officers of the Austrian government'. Nationalism may be an ugly word today, but details like these bring home the cumbersome motley that Europe was before the nationalist struggles of the last 150 years simplified its political outlines. John Forster Baird came across an interesting example of the transition period in which he lived when the horse-drawn diligence he took from Milan to Brescia was transferred to a truck, which was then attached to a train for the only section of the Milan–Venice railway already completed (he noted with interest the English rolling-stock used – 'the well known names of "Thorpe and Roberts"' on an engine in Padua station).

Frontier checks could be quite arbitrary. Customs officers might remove passports, as a moustachioed officer at the Prussian frontier did (promising to forward them on the next train), or scarcely glance at them; boxes could be left untouched or 'turned over' as the officers of the King of Sardinia are graphically described as doing on the Italian border. These incidents were noted, because this was an account for a family at home who had never travelled abroad, so every detail was of interest. They were not a cause of complaint, rather the reverse. Through our traveller's rosy spectacles even the inconveniences added piquant charm to the journey.

The real point about the trip was the freedom it gave him to do the things he liked best: the walks, the sight-seeing, the diverting contact with strangers and the solitude. He 'took' sketches at every stopping point and often left the diligence, which would stop in villages, to make a short-cut by mountain path while it lurched and trundled its way round the hairpin bends. In the evenings, after table d'hôte at an inn, he would walk through the gathering dusk perhaps to the next village and back. Distance was no threat; a six-mile walk was an after-dinner stroll. The diary is full of ecstatic accounts of the scenery: 'One of the most matchless scenes in the world' (of the Gondo valley, south of the Simplon); 'I don't think I ever saw a more beautiful view' (from the top of the Albis, in Switzerland). At Interlaken he went on a moonlit walk towards the Lauterbrunner valley: 'Sky without a cloud and the bold and vast outlines of the mountains gave a grandeur to the scene which it is impossible ever to forget.' He used everyday language to describe feelings about scenes which his one-time school colleague Matthew Arnold would two years later, on his European tour, express in verse:

> *Fast, fast by my window*
> *The rushing winds go*
> *Towards the ice-cumber'd gorges,*
> *The vast fields of snow.*
> *There the torrents drive upward,*

Their rock-strangled hum,
And the avalanche thunders
The hoarse torrents dumb,
I come, O ye mountain –
Ye torrents, I come!

John Forster Baird's sketch of the Gemmi Pass in Switzerland (on the front cover) bears comparison with this early Arnold poem. Both were the experimental offerings of young men bowled over by the dramatic beauty of the Alps. The difference between the two men was that Matthew Arnold went on to work at his art and become one of the leading poets of his age, while John Forster Baird's talent remained, as it had begun, a prolific but private passion.

The Grand Tour was not complete without Italy. The night before he crossed the Simplon he was attacked 'tooth and nail' by bedbugs in the Poste Inn at Brig and had only a few hours' sleep before the horn of the diligence roused its passengers at three in the morning. But early starts were part of this way of life. What we would think of as physical discomforts – bumpy roads, badly sprung carriages – were probably barely noticeable at the time, while a headache (he had a bad one for several days before the Simplon ascent) simply had to be ignored. Though the wildness of the Alps was his first love, one that he would return to again and again in his life, the 'soft beauty of Italy' which it gave way to as they approached Domodossola offered a kind of relief. He walked up the road after dinner to take a sketch, noting the Italianness of the town, 'the streets strongly redolent of macaroni and rotten fruit' and bright with the 'coats of many colours worn by the men and women', the national costume donned by the local inhabitants for their evening stroll along the main street.

At Milan the artistic part of the tour began. They approached

across 'vast fields of grain adorned with vines and mulberry trees
. . . as far as the eye could see', then 'suddenly and without the
slightest preparation, as if by magic we found ourselves at the
entrance of a magnificent avenue of sycamores at the other end
of which a full mile off was to be seen an arch of white marble
of colossal dimensions. These were the first intimations that we
were drawing near to the far-famed and magnificent city of
Milan. . . . When we arrived at the Porte our passports were
taken, and strong symptoms of desire to see our luggage were
shown by the officers in waiting who, however, did not hesitate
to receive a silver bribe and permit us to pass on.'

Ensconced in the Hôtel de la Ville he planned his day. The
Duomo first, followed by the Ambrosian Library, then
Leonardo's 'Last Supper', finally a look-in on La Scala. He spent
a whole morning at the Duomo, and having said he would not
describe it proceeds to do so in considerable detail. Later on in
the Ambrosian Library he pored over Leonardo drawings and
Raphael sketches but makes no comment beyond recording he
has seen them. The 'Last Supper', he noted, would soon be
obliterated – 'yet the effect of the outline which is still preserved
is very wonderful'. Then, after a five a.m. start, he went on to
Venice, via Brescia (where he sketched a ruined amphitheatre)
and Verona.

Verona delighted him. It takes up nine pages of the journal,
starting with the 11-hour journey by 'voiture' for the 50 miles
from Brescia. He stopped and dined at Peschiera on the way,
worried that his lack of Italian would prevent him getting a good
meal, but a German waiter interpreted for him and persuaded
him to drink the local *vin santo*. The following night he
discovered Valpolicella (mentioned in Pliny, he says). These inn
dinners, laced with the local wines and in the company of local
people, were convivial affairs. John Forster Baird was on his own

now. His companion had stayed in Milan so he was free to travel as he liked; the German waiter with whom he could communicate quite freely opened the way to conversation with his fellow guests.

In Verona he sat in the amphitheatre, under an umbrella, to sketch. Lizards scuttled over the hot stones; some strolling players had put up a wooden theatre in the centre of the arena – '*infandum dictu!*' ('shameful to relate') is his comment: amateur dramatics and Roman remains should not be mixed. This was the same view as that drawn by the son of the Newcastle artist, Miles Richardson, he reminds his readers. So on to Venice, stopping overnight at Vicenza where Palladio's buildings amaze him. One can imagine their appeal to his architectural eye, yet strangely he didn't sketch any, nor did he do any drawings in Venice on this journey. Perhaps the shadow of the Venetian masters proved too much for his tender self-esteem.

He arrived by train, at a temporary station near the head of the Grand Canal (the railway was very new) and took a private gondola, as opposed to the omnibus-gondola, 'not wishing to have all sentimental feelings concerning Venice to be done away with at once by making my entry into the city in such an unsentimental conveyance', up the Grand Canal, down a small canal to the Bridge of Sighs then out to the lagoon and to his hotel, the Daniele; then, as now, one of the most expensive in the city.

His journey was a strange mixture. In towns he lived like a lord, in the country he was happy to mix with the locals. His predilection for the village scene in southern Europe, which became more pronounced later, seems to derive not only from his love of dramatic scenery but also from relief at being in an older world, a world where life was still virtually unchanged. Rugby and Cambridge had left him with a mixed identity. He had merged with the southern elite, but his recent origins (only one generation back) were northern provincial, not quite gentry: trade on the Forster side and farming on the Baird. The Tyrolean village was a place he could feel both at home in and free – free from the pressures of 19th-century snobbery.

Venice, where he spent five days (covering 19 pages in his journal) was the climax of his Italian tour. He wrote a guidebook-like summary of it for the family at home, describing gondolas, St Mark's, the Doge's palace, the Armenian monastery (where, he reminds them, Byron studied Armenian), went twice to the Lido, hurrying back to see the pigeons having their 2 p.m. meal in St Mark's Square, visited the Arsenal, churches, looked at pictures – Titians, Tintorettos and Veroneses. You get a wonderful sense of an uncrowded Venice as he tours the almost empty Accademia; the crowds are all at the Rialto, in the vegetable market, where melons are sold for twopence each. At the end of his last day, there is 'one of the most glorious sunsets I ever beheld'. He is back on form: the superlatives are a kind of possessiveness, they make it his place through the sense of specialness they bestow.

But he was not alone any more. A Rugby master, Mr Cotton, whom he had met in Milan, had joined him; then when Cotton left there was an Oxford man (not named) staying at the same hotel who went sightseeing with him. You get an impression of the south of Europe buzzing with English tourists. This was the latest middle-class craze in the relative calm of the middle years of the century: continental travel. And we see another contradiction in our traveller. He is the gregarious solitary. He needs solitude, he enjoys company. But he has a sanguine nature. Whatever time and the hour throw up, he goes along with it. Life happens to him; he is not a great rebel or risk-taker – he is too easy-going. It must have made him a pleasant travelling companion.

His plan had been to return to Milan and go back from there

more or less retracing the outward route. But in Milan he bumped into another friend of his, Richard Hoare, who was travelling with a friend of his, one Hanbury. Hanbury and Hoare persuaded him to go with them to Como and from there north through the Tyrol to Vienna and ultimately Hamburg. He fell in with their plans willingly. Then, in the company of two friends his own age, we see him for the first time in something of a laddish mood. He was no longer the respectful English traveller seeking the help of locals and enjoying their company. Now suddenly he was one of three representatives of a ruling class indulging in a slanging match (at Colico on the north of Lake Como) with a landlady over the price of brandy. He had surely been overcharged before; but Hanbury and Hoare, spotting it, were having none of it and bellowed at the landlady in English while she shouted at them in Italian and the villagers looked on. Hardly the kind of scene our traveller would relish, but he puts it in the diary because it will raise a smile at home. But there is a sense of him distancing himself from his friends – little hints, like when he went out to explore the hillside above their Como hotel in the heat of the day (and take a sketch), leaving them to laze inside. He had his own agenda, and without making a fuss about it, very amiably, was going to stick to it.

We know nothing about that return journey. Those are the missing chapters. It is a pity, as he had his first sight of the Tyrol then, which later he was to explore, path by path, mountain by mountain, till he knew it so well he could write a guidebook about it. Perhaps this 1846 journal should be seen as a prototype of those later guides or as a reconnoitre: he was finding out for the future, the next and subsequent years, how best to do it again – where to go, when and with whom.

Four of them went the next time, in fact, and that was the following year. There was his friend Newman Hall, now with a wife, and John Forster Baird's sister, Jane. Brother and sister, husband and wife set off from Hull on July 7th 1847. They planned to go Milan and back in six weeks. After a night's crossing they reached Rotterdam and soon were headed towards the Rhine – trains had improved in the intervening year. There were the usual customs delays at the Prussian border, but it gave a chance to sketch Emmerich cathedral. The pattern of the journey was going to be very similar to the previous year's; and yet, in important ways, it was different.

In the first place, as they were four persons, more weight had to be given to the group: he and Newman Hall would go out, or John Forster Baird would go on his own to sketch (he was the only one, it seems, who was not afraid of the heat), then later in the day some entertainment would be devised for the ladies – a drive or a trip on the lake. In Zurich they escaped on to the lake to avoid the dust and noise of soldiers marching to music and carrying banners protesting against the Sonderbund, or union of catholic cantons, thus missing the chance to take in the political tension that was gripping Switzerland and which would lead, after a civil war later that year, to a more liberal constitution in 1848. Political landscapes were not part of the Baird itinerary.

It was a journey of nostalgia as much as of discovery. John Forster Baird had the pleasure of returning to old haunts: the same Freiburg hotel where the commissionaire this time gave him a book of his poems. (Did he give the commissionaire a sketch in return? He does not mention it and he probably didn't, not out of meanness, but out of shyness: there is a sense of a lifelong undervaluing of his own work.) Sometimes the pressure of the company became too much and after one crowded lake trip they 'got very hot, very cross and very dusty'. The men at least could take their short or long cuts by mountain path, sometimes walking 10 or 15 miles and catching up with the others later in the day. The ladies meanwhile would be cooped up in the carriage or waiting at a wayside inn; the diary does not relate how they fared.

There was no shortage of distractions along the route. The journal, like the previous year's, is an excellent guide to natural phenomena. Hot springs, chasms, waterfalls (they visited Rheinfall, the source of the Rhine, and the Reichenbach Falls) are all described in detail, as in one of those postcards that superimposes printed information over a splendid view. Witness his account of the view from the top of the Rigi, above Lucerne. He must have stood there with a local guide who pointed out the different landmarks; John Forster Baird transcribed the names phonetically which makes some of them hard to trace.

Below us was the Lake of Lucerne with the Lakes of Sarnen and the Jungfrau behind it and the town of Lucerne itself backed by the huge Pilatus, beyond this the snowy peaks of the Bernese Alps and the groups of the Fluhli and St Gotthard. In the east were the Ingersten and Rissley, the little Lake of Lauerzer, half cloaked with the debris of the mountain, the Muotatal and in the distance the Alps of Glarner and Appenzall. In the north the Lake of Zurich was just visible, the Albi and the comparatively level country of northern Switzerland. At one part on the same side lay the lake and town of Zug, the former the brightest blue it is possible to conceive.

This was all aimed at the Newcastle drawing-room with its audience who would never see these marvels themselves. It was a verbal panorama which would both inform them and kindle their imaginations.

But the tone of this journal is subtly different from the previous year's. John Forster Baird was in charge, he made all the bookings (hotels, voitures, guides) but it was his companions' itinerary he followed and it left him with little time for journalizing (even his output of sketches was affected) other than the daily factual record, written at great speed with many slips of the pen. After they had left Milan and were heading north again (where, near Como, they passed a thief in the stocks), the Newman Halls decided to go their own way. For the last week of the holiday the Baird siblings were left on their own; and now it is clear that Jane (who, according to my eldest aunt, would inappropriately wear her best boots on Bamburgh beach, and as we know had that dreadful trouble with her dying feet) was almost as stalwart a walker as her brother. Day after day they set off on long mountain treks, often through foul weather and occasionally losing their way. I said that John Forster Baird was not a risk-taker. In his art he did not have what Kipling, in *The Light That Failed*, calls 'the conviction that nails the work to the wall', but he had plenty of courage when it came to tackling a mountain trail in a thunderstorm against the advice of people (in this case French walkers near Interlaken) who had just tried it.

'Take a knapsack and stick, walk towards the hills by short days' journeys – ten or twelve miles a day . . . sleep at the pretty wayside inns, or the rough village ones; then take the hills as they tempt you. . . . Gradually the deeper scenes of the natural world will unfold themselves to you . . . and your difficulty will be no more to seek or to compose subjects, but only to choose one from among the multitude.' Thus Ruskin recommended in his *Elements of Drawing*, published in1857. Ten years earlier John Forster Baird was doing just that. His diaries may be full of conveyances and voitures but his portfolios show mountain scenery it must have taken hours of walking to reach, through the 'deeper scenes of the natural world'. I have a picture of his in front of me as I write. It is of Achensee in the Tyrol, a sketch done in 1863 (on one of the holidays mentioned in the list made for the dying Gertrude). It is drawn in black chalk with touches of white body colour. It shows, opposite a small lakeside chapel and gleaming belfry, a farmhouse-chalet with traditional overhanging eaves and roof tiles weighted down with stones. There is a gleam of summer haze over the whole; one can smell the warm valley air under the shadowy stillness of the huge mountains that circle the lake. The picture is undramatic and understated, as all his sketches are; but there is an intimacy about it, an inner intensity, that make it easy to imagine the discarded knapsack and propped stick as the artist leans against a boulder and breathes in the scene before he starts to draw.

A few months after his return from this second continental tour, John Forster Baird did a painting of a shipwreck off Dunstanburgh, on the Northumbrian coast. A sailing ship is impaled on the rocks, with waves breaking over it and foam flying; Dunstanburgh castle gleams in the distance under a tempestuous sky, while smoke rises from a fire signal on the shore. It is an unusually strong picture, reminiscent of some of the more dramatic works of the Newcastle watercolourists. But its artist had got his place in the Inner Temple by then. His future path was charted. This homage to Dunstanburgh was, I feel, a last fling before the Bar closed round him.

Other things too were pressing in on him. Perhaps it was the presence of the recently married Newman Halls that reminded him what the single young man with a large fortune should be looking for; perhaps it was his sister's company that made him crave a more sympathetic female walking-companion (Jane was a ceaseless talker). Whatever it was that readied him for it, sometime before or after the turn of the decade as he was approaching his 30th birthday, he met and fell in love with Emily Brinton, an energetic, strikingly handsome 22-year-old with eyes as blue as the lake at Zug and a love of abroad, the Tyrol in particular, almost equal to his own.

5   *The Brinton Connection*

*You may go to the Bar, and become distinguished; . . . you
may lawfully keep several hundred men, women and
children at work for twelve hours a day in your
unwholesome factory, and then you may become wealthy
and influential and erect public baths and patronise artists.*
Tom Arnold to his mother, 1847

In the sardonic letter quoted above, Matthew Arnold's younger
brother Tom highlighted two of the routes that might be taken
by the contemporary professional man. Tom in fact went down
neither path, neither into the Bar nor into factory ownership.
John Forster Baird chose the first as his career, and married into
the second.

Emily Brinton, the young lady with the blue eyes, was the
youngest of eight children, the fourth daughter of Henry Brinton,
a carpet manufacturer of Kidderminster. The family connection
with cloth went back two centuries. They had produced five
generations of weavers and dyers before Emily's grandfather,
William Brinton, bought three-quarters of an acre of land outside
Kidderminster in the 1770s and set up the family weaving
business there. It was an auspicious moment to launch out. The
industrial revolution was pushing up standards of living among
the wealthy classes. The Brintons were manufacturing one of the
key commodities that soon every householder in the land would

be wanting: carpets. Carpets to keep out the draughts, carpets to cover rough floorboards, carpets to hang on your walls, even to drape over your occasional tables.

Those 'crossed' love letters referred to in Chapter 1, whose transcription by my great-aunt released me from the sense of eavesdropping on the secrets of my ancestors, were written by Henry Brinton, Emily's father. Though a detail in our story, they are an important one, for two reasons. They provide a keyhole view on a marital scene which is repeated, with almost poetic symmetry, at the end of our tale; and they give us a telling glimpse into Emily Brinton's background.

She came from a very different stable from the Bairds. It was puritan, hard-working and high-minded, qualities which of course were present in the Bairds' world, but were elevated to a higher level of importance in the ethos of the new industrialism. Henry Brinton, Emily's father, had married a Dublin girl, Martha Gardiner, in 1817. (The Gardiners were emigrants from England, an unusual phenomenon in the mid-19th century when the slums of London were beginning to fill up with impoverished Irish, but for whatever reason Martha's father had transferred his business, which was cabinet making, to Dublin.) Both before and after their marriage Henry Brinton wrote long and pious crossed letters to Martha which, to begin with at least, were very loving. He had an impatient temperament, he said ('I cannot number patience among my acquirements') and he wooed her with the same single-minded purposefulness with which he pursued his family's business. The following excerpt comes from a letter written before their marriage in 1817, after he had returned home from a trip to Ireland.

Every hour brings it's [sic] duties, and I have had some very laborious ones to perform this morning, as your very welcome epistle found me immersed in a vast ocean of business of almost every kind, though all and everything

I ever received at your hands was sweet to me, yet this was doubly endeared to me, truly it was like a cooling stream in the Sandy deserts of Arabia. . . . Ah, my love, I wish I could fly to you this night. . . . My mind often takes a rapid flight, and fearless of the terrors of the sea which separates the two countries, passes the narrow bound and delights to hover near you.

On the back he transcribed some poems and two hymns, 'The Star of Bethlehem' and 'Praise to the Redeemer'.

This fragile, faded document perfectly typifies the time when it was written, with its romantic language, the evidence of its writer's hard-working life and its religious postscript. This is the age of the work ethic. The Brintons were nonconformists and would have absorbed with their mother's milk (or perhaps later with the schoolmaster's stick) the message that the devil makes work for idle hands.

Martha was four years Henry's senior. Stern-faced and strong-jawed, she stares out at me from a cameo photograph. If I cover the top half of her face (the rather close-set eyes and challenging gaze under an extraordinary bonnet such as the rhinoceroses in *Babar* wore), I see my mother's mouth and jaw. That square Gardiner jaw appears in all the family photographs, though thankfully it is softened in later generations. But Martha proved rough going for Henry – or did he for her? We only have his side of it, in a letter written in September 1820, three years after their marriage:

Believe me, my love, I am not that Severe, Passionate husband nor that hard taskmaster which you have drawn the picture of in your two last letters, nay, I am convinced that in a happier moment you yourself would be proud to say that there is no resemblance in the Portraits – To this decision I leave it, and will only say, that I never followed your example in drawing such an ugly figure and writing your name under it. . . . If I were so blessed as to hear that my speedy return was not indifferent to you, there is no knowing how my progress would be accelerated –

nonetheless I do not wish your lips to express any sentiments which your heart does not echo.

One warms to Henry for that last phrase. Did he really want her to say exactly what she felt? What he called her 'peevish complaints and reproaches' in a letter a year later could have been the desperate response of a spirited woman trapped into repeated pregnancies, left at home by a travelling husband to grapple with the tedious daily round of servants and social constriction. I call her spirited, as that is how I see her in spite of that fierce photograph. Her daughter Emily was full of vitality, just as Emily's daughter, Mary, was. All three of these under-educated, energetic women dealt with the lack of scope for their talents in the same way, by endless handcraft – knitting, sewing, lacework – and having babies. Martha had eight, Emily seven, Mary nine. Of course there was much more going on in their lives, but their identities were defined by motherhood. The sheer size of their families saw to that. But withal the 'glory' of giving birth (and the relief at having survived it and having a living baby) the shock effect of constant pregnancies must have been profound. Add to that the struggle to build a relationship with a man you hardly knew, and you can get some idea of the stress and disillusionment of those first years of marriage after the romantic thrill of courtship and the excitement of the actual ceremony. We meet this scene again, poignantly mirrored two generations later at the end of our story.

In October 1845, when Emily Brinton was 15, her two elder sisters Martha and Sarah had a double wedding. Both girls married into the carpet trade: 24-year-old Martha to Frank Crossley of Halifax and 20-year-old Sarah to Edward Broome (who died four years later). Frank ran his family business, Edward's father was a carpet-manufacturer though he himself was a lawyer. Henry Brinton, the girls' father, had just finished building large new weaving-sheds in the centre of Kidderminster which would later give the firm an edge over its competitors when power-looms came in. But the new labour-saving machines would lead to strikes and, with the exodus of unemployed weavers from the town, a drop in its population which only picked up again after the arrival of the railway and the consequent expansion of business in the early 1850s.

This industrial setting is an important background to our story. The Brinton family's status would later be a key element in my grandmother's life, and therefore indirectly in mine too, since but for it my grandparents would probably not have met. Rich manufacturing families like them occupied a dual role in society, as Tom Arnold so caustically observed. They were the pace-setters of the industrial revolution (Brintons, like Wedgwoods, successfully survived all vicissitudes and are still leaders in their field today), and as such had to make harsh decisions. Searching through sources on women's education in the 1870s, when Mary Baird and her sisters were teenagers, I came across an account of a smart move by John Brinton, Emily's brother and then head of the firm, to employ women instead of men. His motives were obvious: this was in a period of falling profits and women could be paid less than men. The industrial strife that ensued was reported as far afield as France, in *Le Figaro*. But at the same time these hard-headed industrialists were pillars of respectability in their own communities and philanthropists on a grand scale. The Crossleys of Halifax (later of Somerleyton) built alms-houses, a chapel, an orphanage, model housing and a park. The Brintons meanwhile did their bit for Kidderminster with a park and, when the town finally got its own piped water supply in 1870 after a cholera epidemic four years earlier, a fountain. Both families produced mayors and members of Parliament, Whigs, on the liberal wing of the party. And both families took their obligations – social and financial – towards their wider family very seriously.

This, then, was the world the Brinton sisters came from. Two of them had exchanged their parental home for others very similar: luxurious mansions, comfortable incomes, a diet of good works and family prayers before breakfast (which Emily introduced into the Baird household). Both the elder daughters were much loved by their Baird nieces, and Martha Crossley in particular was endowed with a generous nature which made her take on the role of fairy godmother to the less well-off members of her family and her friends. When it came to the turn of Emily, the third daughter, to marry she drew, I was going to say, the short straw; rather let us call it a different one, a very different one.

What would the Brintons have seen when they first met John Forster Baird? A good-looking young man with regular features, blue eyes, light brown hair and perhaps just enough of a trace of Northumbrian lilt to his voice to reassure them he was at heart a creature of the provinces like them. He would have had a sophisticated charm, possibly the slightly self-deprecating smile of the man who knows he will never quite live up to other people's expectations of him, but covering this with the easy manner of the educated traveller, at home in foreign languages and cultures. This would have particularly appealed to Emily's brother William, later a distinguished surgeon and member of the Royal Society, who was to become an active member of an Alpine walking club. The aspiring suitor also had a coat of arms, a private income and a future at the Bar. He was a decidedly suitable husband.

They married in Kidderminster on October 3rd 1854. There

is a charming drawing of the Malvern Hills in John Forster Baird's sketchbook, dated June 23rd 1854, which has both their initials, JFB and EJB (she was Emily Jane), a joint work; and then another one in the same book of Whitley Court, Worcestershire, showing an elegantly dressed lady with a parasol in the foreground who must be Emily. It was very much a love-match, to judge by the letters he wrote to her after their marriage. There was an anecdote, handed down by one of my aunts, about the three married Brinton sisters discussing how they kept their feet warm at night. While the elder sisters' talk was of warming pans, Emily said she warmed her feet against her husband's legs. Evidence of a happy marriage, said my aunt.

They must have made a fine trio, those Brinton girls. Martha, or Aunt Frank, as she was called by her nieces after her husband's Christian name, was born to the role of *grande dame*. Her fine aquiline profile and slightly curved smile greets today's visitors to Somerleyton Hall; it is impossible to look up at that imposing sculpture and not feel slightly in awe of her. Her generosity was impressive, likewise her high moral tone. My mother had a photograph of her. It showed an elegantly dressed Victorian lady – in profile, of course – with a lace snood over straight hair swept up into a chignon. She had the same deep-set eyes as Emily but with a softer look, and the humorous curve of the mouth of the Somerleyton sculpture. It was in an ornate and slightly chipped gold frame, which I mended after my mother's death and hung on my wall, feeling I had breathed a little life into the memory of a beautiful person. Then we had a break-in; the picture was taken. Aunt Frank now graces the wall of a stranger, probably unaware that she is stolen property. I would love to get her back.

Sarah, 'Aunt Broome', is a more shadowy figure. She was much loved by my grandmother but she is only conspicuous in the diaries for her terror of thunderstorms. Emily was without doubt the spikiest of the three (she seems to have inherited a larger share of the Brinton impatience), but also the most adventurous. She did not object to her babies being transported across Alpine passes in panniers strapped to a mule. She made her daughters their dresses (and some of their hats). At the age of 65 she learnt to ride a bicycle; and according to my mother throughout her life had an 18-inch waist. In spite of the damage her stays must have inflicted, she lived till she was 82.

There was a tradition among later Baird descendants that John Forster Baird had married 'down', that trade was below the ranks of the landed gentry to which he supposedly belonged. The roots of this lay in Victorian snobbery, reinforced later, I suspect, by Oxford arrogance. In truth, it could not have been more wide of the mark. John Forster Baird made, by accident or design (more likely the first), a very canny move. Any temporary downward social mobility was more than offset by his connection with the rising Crossleys. Frank Crossley would soon be made a baronet and acquire the large estate at Somerleyton Hall where his widow's effigy presides today. The growing Baird family was to find frequent sanctuary there – and my grandmother her future husband.

The Crossley mantle spread over the young Baird couple from the start; Belle Vue, their Halifax house, became a second home to Emily whenever her John was away or she needed a bit of cosseting. The Bairds had begun their married life in Newcastle, in Bentinck Villas, Elswick, an airy suburb well away from the grimy centre of town. It was there just over a year later, on December 3rd 1855, that my grandmother Mary was born. John Forster Baird meanwhile set up chambers in Westgate Street and waited for briefs, at first with no result, then suddenly with more than he could handle: 'Isn't it very odd that after waiting patiently 4 months without anything to do I should be

73

detained [from joining Emily in Halifax] by briefs,' he wrote in July 1855. He missed her enormously when she was away: 'I am very dull in the evenings. I love you very much.'

He was becoming a family man. The baby, or babies (a second daughter, Emmie, was born in March 1857), were mentioned in every letter; and letters flowed between him and Emily whenever they were separated. These were not long missives, more like the telephone calls of today, dealing with immediate things like who they had just seen and what they would be doing the next day. From these letters, lovingly preserved by Emily after her husband's death, you can see the centre of gravity of John Forster Baird's life gradually shifting. Law, whether through lack of briefs or of interest, is soon pushed into the background. His concern is property: first the search for somewhere for them to live after they decide to move to London, and then the overseeing of his patrimony, the source of his income, in the north.

His uncle William, his father's brother and co-legatee of the wealthy William Baird of Alnwick, acted as John Forster Baird's agent. There is a letter from him, dated 1851, which gives a graphic picture of the nitty-gritty husbandry involved in this job of looking after his nephew's estates. We are back with Northumbrian earth again, but this time drainage is the theme. Uncle William Baird has spent £1,660 for building and drainage on his nephew's land, and wants some of it back. 'When the Tile Bills and Drainers Accts comes in I shall be running my cash acct hard up to a close with the Bank and having advanced on acct to you £25 towards Rands half year rent I would like to retain the other part for a few months in case you can conveniently do without it if not you can let me know. . .' The letter flows on without punctuation. This is the authentic Baird voice before any expensive school or university has polished it;

and very friendly it is. John Forster Baird has sent his uncle some booze: 'I received the Gin safe and is very good it often puts me in mind of the good gin we got in that blind publick house just before leaving by the steamer from London.' You can hear Uncle William's chuckle as he remembers the 'blind' public house. We will meet him again. He was childless, and his demise, a generation later, was to change the family's fortunes as much as his earlier namesake's had done his, but with more tragic consequences.

John Forster Baird could not delegate all his business to his uncle. There were rents to be renegotiated, new leases for tenants which only he could arrange, involving frequent visits north, particularly in the shooting and fishing season. In the late 1850s he was trying to persuade the Duke of Northumberland to buy one of his farms, St Margaret's, but first a hefty £300 had to be spent on it. The following excerpts from a letter he wrote to Emily, in November 1860, give an idea of the pressures on him.

If the Duke gives the terms Mr Taylor said were fair for St Margaret's I shall have no difficulty about the Piano, back Drawing Room curtains and new Chintz which would make us quite smart again, but I must not be too sanguine about this, as it is very possible he may not buy, and the place in the general market would be nearly unsaleable. . . . I enclose £5 out of which give Jane and Anna [his sisters] something if they require it. . . . I have not heard of you and the spots [babies] for two days – shall I get a letter tomorrow?'

He was supporting his two unmarried sisters; he was being pressed by Emily to refurbish their home and buy a piano. If all his father's capital had been invested in bonds he would have had a steady £300 a year (£15,000 at today's value), not that much, and his income was probably mostly in the form of rents from properties that needed endless reinvestment. One imagines the Forster-Baird wealth came in fits and starts: there were good years and bad. It must have been very tempting to realize lump sums by selling off assets, as he was trying to do in getting the Duke of Northumberland to buy one of his farms. Mary later recalled that one of her earliest memories was the sound of her parents arguing about money. Who took the lead – Emily, upbraiding her husband for not earning enough, or he her for spending too much?

In October 1856 they signed a lease on 34 Belgrave Road, in Pimlico, London. It was a joint family move. Brother William and his wife and the two Baird sisters moved in with them. With four floors (four reception and eight bedrooms) there was room for them all. The rent was £75 a year, plus taxes of £12 6s. It was part of the Thomas Cubitt development of Pimlico, built in the 1830s, rudely dismissed as 'Stuccoville' by one late Victorian, but to our 21st-century eyes an elegant area of well-proportioned houses suggestive of everything the Bairds stood for: ample enough means and overflowing nurseries. John Forster Baird was much relieved to have found it after several months' intensive house-hunting. You hear his satisfaction in this postscript to a letter to Emily, shortly before they moved in: 'Love to babe [Mary, then ten months] – I should like to have her opinion of the House and of a day nursery 18 ft by 20 ft.'

Mary, writing about it later, by which time she had clearly forgotten her palatial day nursery, did not mince her words: 'a most unattractive spot I thought it when once I passed by.' It was lucky she had not been more conscious of her environment when she was pushed – or carried – through the streets of Pimlico by her nanny, Atty (Alice Johnson, the Northumbrian girl we met at John Baird's deathbed). At the bottom of Belgrave Road ran the Thames, where the sewer that was the outlet for the mod. con. appliances in the smart Cubitt houses debouched.

In June 1858 occurred what became known as 'the Great Stink', when the stench from these outlets was so obnoxious that pedestrians crossing Westminster Bridge had to hold handkerchiefs to their noses.

In June 1858, though, the Bairds were abroad, as they had been every other summer since they married. John Forster Baird's sketches chart their movements. In April 1858 they were in Bex; in July in Interlaken; in August by the Lake of Lucerne. In October 1858 a third daughter, Gertrude (Doty), was born. Emily had spent the middle months of her pregnancy traipsing around Europe with her husband and the two other little girls (that was the pannier holiday). She seems to have taken to this way of life with alacrity, which was lucky. She was married to a man who, though he had set himself up in chambers in the Temple, preferred the rifle range to the office, the grouse moors to the shooting range and travel – plus sketchbook – to any of these. Perhaps the frequent neuralgia Emily suffered from on their journeys was a protest against those nomadic summers. Matthew Arnold, contemplating a foreign holiday with his family in 1857, worried how they would manage it: 'What to do with the 3 children is too embarrassing,' he wrote. But children – three, four or more – were no embarrassment to John Forster Baird, and Emily just had to accept it. There is a telling letter from a Corbridge friend of hers (the signature is missing) written in May 1857. The family had just arrived on the continent; they had had a rough journey, and John Forster Baird's health was not all it should have been.

My dear Mrs Baird,   May 28
   We were very glad to hear of you again and only wish you could have reported better of your husband. But I have always heard that a little blood may be spit, from many causes beside lung disease and the fact that there

has been no return of this symptom and that since it occurred he has grown stronger [allows] great hope that nothing serious is the matter. I pity you travelling with your two babes, for with children one cannot so bravely encounter rough seas and the ups & downs of foreign parts, but still if it is necessary it must be done.

Necessary it seemed to be. The Baird income would go further on the continent where rents, food and labour were all cheaper (some 15 years earlier Charles Dickens had found his household expenses halved when he took his family to Italy). But reports of these ups and downs must have reached Kidderminster. In that same year, barely two months before the Bairds were on their way to the continent with their two babes, Emily's father, Henry Brinton, had died. He was 61; the cause of death was registered as 'natural decay'. The Brinton business passed to his eldest son, another Henry, who was himself to die six months later. Emily was left £600 (£30,000 today), to be invested in government bonds or railway stock, the income from it to be 'for her sole and separate use free from the debts control & engagements' of her husband. This was a formula, in point of fact a legally invalid one: until the Married Women's Property Act of 1870 husbands had complete control over their wives' assets unless they were protected by a trust (and this legacy was not). But the wording perhaps indicates Henry's concern at his son-in-law's unorthodox lifestyle. A naturally worried man, there must have been moments when he feared for his daughter's future.

Meanwhile, the Pimlico menage was breaking up. 'The dreary house in Belgrave Road must have been the scene of many family discords,' wrote Mary later, with a certain mischievous satisfaction. In 1860 William was ordained and moved out with his wife to an East End parish, taking his sisters with him. John Forster Baird was left in sole possession of the house.

For some, London in the 1860s was an exciting place to live.

There was plenty of diversion for the well-off citizen. It was the great age of the music hall; theatres were beginning to offer upmarket entertainment such as Charles Fechter's *Hamlet* in the new 'realistic' style or a farce with music by Arthur Sullivan. The Baird letters and diaries do not mention any theatre-going, but John Forster Baird had a liking for theatricals and it was a period when talented amateurs were encouraged to try their luck on the professional stage. In the late 1850s he had done just that, making his first and only foray into the world of professional theatre. It is a strange story, of the barrister–artist momentarily turning playwright, and it has a dramatic twist, like a moment in a Russian novel when two characters whom destiny will later link pass each other by, unaware of what the future will hold.

The protagonists were John Forster Baird and Henry Irving, later the greatest actor of his generation; the scene, the Sunderland Lyceum; the year, 1856. John Forster Baird had written the libretto for a burlesque to be performed at the opening of the newly rebuilt Lyceum. The burlesque, 'a highly successful New Piece of Oriental Sentimentality or Sentimental Orientality, extracted from the dreams of the Arabian Nights' (in relentless rhyming couplets laced with puns), was to be the warm-up before the serious business of the evening, Bulwer Lytton's *Richelieu*, with a prologue spoken by the young Henry Irving in his first ever professional appearance. Irving in fact appeared in both plays, acting the part of cook in the burlesque. Did he and John Forster Baird meet in the bar between acts? If they had, and if some emissary of the gods had tweaked their elbows and introduced them to each other as future joint fathers-in-law, they might have blinked. But that is what they were to be. John Forster Baird's daughter, Dolly, and Irving's son, H.B. Irving, both went on the stage, met and later married. But this would be 40 years hence, and over 15 years after John Forster

Baird himself had died. On that evening in Sunderland neither of the children in question had been dreamt of, let alone born, and if the two men did clink glasses their meeting passed unnoticed.

The story, though, affords us another insight into John Forster Baird's diffuse life. He had rented chambers in London for his conveyancing, but the law could not hold his interest. He was also spending time at the rifle range on Wimbledon Common; and I think it is reasonable to infer that the 20-foot drawing room in Pimlico with its chintz curtains and piano would have been the scene of many an amateur theatrical.

Overriding all this was the need to economize; and this soon made its mark on the Baird way of life. Winter and spring were given over to work and entertainment in London; summer and autumn to travel and painting, in the north (Bamburgh) or abroad.

Early 1864 they gave up the Pimlico house and moved into temporary accommodation in Richmond, Surrey. The sewers probably helped the decision. The children were not thriving in the polluted London air. Furthermore, the rent of the Pimlico house now fell on John Forster Baird alone. By giving it up nearly £100 a year could be saved, while if they went abroad after a winter in Richmond they would not have to rent another property until the following autumn. Thus for some six months after their brief Richmond stay (which saw the birth of a fourth daughter, Lilian) the Baird family were on their travels again, this time without any English base at all.

The children, snug in their panniers on the mule's back, knew nothing of this. Emily could get some comfort from her sister Martha Crossley's solid status and open house which would be there for them whenever they returned. John Forster Baird, meanwhile, seemed to have no further shadows on his lungs or on his mind as his beloved mountains approached. Yet that short phrase, 'a little blood may be spit', suddenly puts a new complexion on his Alpine obsession. John Keats had seen the first spot of blood on his pillow as the harbinger of death. With his family medical history, John Forster Baird must have known a spit of blood could be ominous. Where better to throw off the disease's dread tentacles than in the pure air and soul-lifting beauty of the Alps?

6   *The Nomad Years*

Much travel is injurious to the soul.
  Mary Baird, in her Swiss diary, October 11 1872

Mary has her story, her parents theirs. We have three versions
of hers (her diaries during the family travels, a short reminiscence
of her childhood which she wrote later in life, and the chapter
in her biography of her husband where she describes it). Her
parents' side of the story we can deduce from his and his wife's
published work. It is this that I will start with.

In 1865 John Forster Baird wrote a guidebook, *Bradshaw's
Illustrated Hand Book to the Tyrol*. He updated the subsequent
editions for about 15 years; I have his proof copies for 1865,
1875 and 1879. Bound in red leather with gold lettering under
a lion-and-unicorn crest, they exude the slightly musty smell of
a Victorian study or the inside of a knapsack. The 1865 volume
is slim enough to slip inside the pocket of a mackintosh (those
useful waterproof coats which had come into fashion in the late
1830s). It is printed in double columns and contains
descriptions of over two dozen routes, twelve to fifty miles long,
with full details of the roads and short (or long) cuts, local
beauty spots, convenient stopping points and the various means
of transport. There is also a programme of longer recommended
tours, from two to six weeks, and a list of summer wild flowers

and where to find them (this was Emily's contribution). Each route has its map showing footpaths as well as roads. The backpacker is catered for as well as the more formal traveller: 'The expenses of pedestrians in the Tyrol, who don't mind carrying their own knapsack, are very trifling, and need not exceed 35 to 50 shillings per week.' For the fainter hearted there are '*vetturini* [private carriages] . . . generally exorbitant', the *stelwagen* at a penny a mile, the faster *postwagen,* the four-person *eilwagen* or the one-horse *einspan* – and of course the train. With all this choice of transport one imagines Tyrolean roads echoing to the rattle of wagons and the sound of the post-horn, but in fact it was an unfrequented region. Unlike Switzerland, which already 'belonged' to so many other northern visitors, the Tyrol could give travellers a real sense of discovery; and as in his earlier journals, this is what John Forster Baird manages to communicate in this book. His enthusiasms break through the terse text. We pass through a charming village, 'a worthy subject for the pencil of the artist'; we look back at a 'strikingly beautiful view', we climb up to splendid heights from where we can see 'the most interesting old town imaginable'. Here is a passage taken from 'Route 5, from Mals to Bormio in the Valentine':

Eight miles from Prad is the village of Trafoi, where the post-house will on an emergency (in which it is not infrequently tested) supply twenty beds. Though the fare is homely, travellers may very pleasantly spend a few days here in exploring the many sights of this most romantic of valleys. A little gallery at the back of the inn commands a fine view of the valley of the three springs from which the name Trafoi or Trefoi (*ad Tres Fontes*) is derived. A path leads from the back of the inn over the meadows and through fir-woods to a little chapel a short distance from the foot of the glacier, by the side of which *Rhododendron hirsutum*, more brilliant in colour than that commonly called the Alpenrose (*Rhododendron ferrugineum*), grows in great profusion. Opposite to the chapel three waterfalls of nearly equal height are seen issuing from openings in the rocks below the Madatsch Spitz. The scene at this point is quite unequalled for savage grandeur; indeed, the view from the shores of the See-alp-see in Appenzall is almost its only parallel.

The author has travelled these Tyrolean routes himself, every inch of the way. He has hired the local guides to take him across glaciers, stayed at the mountain inns, sampled the local wines, seen the ruined castles (still unrepaired after the Napoleonic war), made notes on their history and sketched them for the illustrations in the book. This is his story of those years, the love story behind these long journeys which kept him serene whatever their discomforts, but which wore out his eldest daughter as the latest baby grizzled and the nanny passed her over to the lap of young Mary because her own legs ached.

Mary's memories, not surprisingly, give a different picture. Here is her account of a typical journey: 'An early start, at 4 am, and we 4 or 5 [children] all ready and uncomplaining, perhaps sitting for hours in crowded and smelly railway-carriages, or in the seats of uncomfortable vehicles with our bare legs dangling and often bleeding, the prey of horse-flies.' For her father, she realized that all this travel was 'pure joy', and for her mother, too, 'really fun'. But during one of these alternate summers abroad (a summer which could last from May till November), the elder children were sent to three day schools, in Vevey, Berchtesgaden and Stuttgart, and the family lodged in up to six different hotels or chalets on the trip. Mary, as the eldest, bore more than her share of the nursery responsibilities. As soon as she was old enough her mother would use her as nurse-maid. In Florence, where they stayed over the winter of 1864–5, while her parents spent the evenings with a group of friends which included the Tom Trollopes (Anthony's brother and his wife), and put on theatricals to raise money for one of their number who could not afford the fare home – and where the vivacious Emily with her fashionable clothes and wasp-waist attracted more attention than her husband liked – Mary would stay at home with Atty to dandle a restless baby and walk it to sleep up and down the cold tiled floor of their lodgings.

There were of course moments of fun for Mary, too, and the other two older girls. But Atty's regime was a puritanical one. There were to be no games played, and no soap used on Sundays; and the northern nanny was deeply distrustful of Italy with its incense-filled churches. But she was getting old (she had a stroke while they were staying in Berchtesgaden). As a result of Atty's illness and their mother's preoccupation with her social life, the children were very much left to their own devices. In Vevey they met a group of American boys who were boarding in the nearby Pension Sillig and who spied on the Baird girls – the 13-year-old Mary, 12-year-old Emmie and Gertrude, not quite ten – as they played in the garden of their green-shuttered house beside the lake. The three girls must have been an arresting sight with their fair hair flowing down their backs. Later on these untamed locks were to get them into trouble at their Stuttgart school: their mother wanted them left loose but the school insisted on braids, so the children would plait them hurriedly on their way to school. It was at the Stuttgart school that they learnt the German *schrift*, the Gothic script in use at the time, singing a rhythmical chant in time with the up-and-down strokes of their spluttery pens as they shaped the letters. (And it was in *schrift* that Mary wrote an angry letter to Hitler some 75 years later during the Second World War which, not surprisingly, he never answered.)

In Stuttgart too they had the excitement of the funeral of the school's *Rektor* (head), when all the schoolgirls had to walk across his grave on a plank singing '*Alle Menschen mussen sterben*'

(Everyone must die). 'Like Mr Polly, I never enjoyed a funeral so much!' was Mary's later comment.

The naughty, mischievous moments were the ones she remembered enjoying most – like playing 'mass' in Berchtesgaden with their landlady's son who had a priest's kit, or Christmas Day in Vevey when those same American boys came round with a bunch of mistletoe and turned out the lights.

Mary was beginning to define herself as a rebel, and not just when they were abroad. When, six months after the Berchtesgaden episode, the family were staying with the Crossleys in Halifax, she smuggled a bottle of melted liquorice into the Congregational chapel where her aunt had taken her and shared it with her cousin Savile Crossley, 18 months her junior, to enliven the sermon and endless prayers.

During those early years the symbol of law and order in the household was not Atty or their parents, but the current governess. Halifax provided a particularly lethal specimen, a Miss M., who was prone to violent fits of temper. When Miss M. fell into a river on a picnic the children watched with mixed feelings as the current bore her away ('We all stood aghast, but not quite shocked enough, I fear,' wrote Mary in her *Life of A.L. Smith*). The governess's bustle bore her up ('she floated gaily and was at once pulled out'), thus living to chide them another day. After Miss M., whose photograph still 60 years later evoked in Mary memories she would 'wish to lose', there was Fraulein Duncker, a governess recruited on their travels. Fraulein Duncker helped them keep up their German but hated fresh air and particularly hated Bamburgh (where air comes fresher than in most places). Then there was a Miss Selle, believed by the children to be an atheist because she introduced them to Shelley (the Baird parents did not seem to mind); and she was followed by others whose names have not been recorded. Finally there was Thilda from Bavaria, whom we met in the 1871 census, who for a while – almost – became a member of the family.

The role of governess was an ambiguous one, as that of au pairs can be today. To what extent were you a member of the family, on which side of the invisible green baize door did you belong? However much you were supposedly part of the family it was, after all, a low-status job. When a middle-class nursery full of girls had to be educated and their future considered, this was one career path (the Jane Eyre route) parents like the Bairds would never for a second contemplate for their own children. There was a slight blurring of roles in the Baird family; Emily had originally taught her own children reading, writing and music, and as soon as Mary and Emmie were old enough they were expected to take on the role of tutor to the little ones. The Halifax dragon had been a proper, full-time governess; but the task of the later ones was almost entirely limited to that of language teacher, while the elder girls looked after the basic education. Perhaps John Forster Baird could feel grateful that he did not have a son. This was indeed education on the cheap.

But through the pores of their skin the children were absorbing rich life experiences during all this travel, a process that could not strictly be called education, but nonetheless had a highly educational effect and rounded their personalities. In Mary's case it made her confident to the point of wilfulness and gave her great social poise; and it made her yearn for a firmer base to her life, an anchor, human or spiritual, to tether it to.

The first anchor she found, and one which in fact lasted all her life, was religion. This girl who had played at mass and loved a good funeral and only kept going during Congregational prayers by sucking liquorice-sticky fingers, experienced not quite a road-to-Damascus conversion (as a good Victorian she was steeped in religion already) but a sudden coming together of the different parts of her life – beliefs, emotions, attachments – into one whole that made sense of everything. It happened in the late 1860s, on one of the summers not spent abroad, at Bamburgh.

We have to imagine her on a Sunday evening, sitting in the church. She is in her mid-teens; simply dressed, with some sort of unfussy bonnet that doesn't completely hide her shiny fair hair loosely tied back in a snood. She has a face that people love to look at for its bright eyes (her mother's blue) and its ready smile. She knows she is considered a beauty but perhaps because her mind is always actively engaged on one complicated thought or another she does not have space for vanity – that is not one of her failings. Her problem now is how to be Christianly good, something she has often thought about but without ever convincing herself she can be. Now, in this ancient church with the candles flickering and the Norman pillars gleaming, it suddenly seems possible. It was in this church, she said, that she first learnt the value of prayer, or first believed it would be answered. In a word, her soul found peace.

It was no accident that this happened at Bamburgh, that Baird/Forster matrix. Mary could sit in the church, sensing the ghosts of her forebears, aware that the small Northumbrian community around her were kith, if not all kin. The current vicar, the Rev. William Darnell, was a family friend, the Darnell and Baird children playmates, and Mr Darnell a follower of the 'advanced [Oxford] movement' as Mary calls it. He allowed coloured vestments in church, candles, processions, music – everything in fact that made religion attractive to the senses as well as to the spirit. The fact that Mary's mother had temporarily fallen under the spell of low-church evangelicalism while they were staying in Switzerland perhaps helped push Mary towards high-church practices. There was not much scope for teenage rebellion in the 19th century, but religion, with all its welter of different rituals, could provide an acceptable conduit for it.

For each of their Bamburgh visits the Bairds rented Wynding House, a 17th-century farmhouse within sight of the castle and sound of the sea. It was lived in by the Dixon family, tenants of the castle and relatives of the Darlings whose famous daughter, Grace, with her big marble effigy in the church, was practically a local saint. What struck Mary on their first visit, though, was the alarming appearance of Grace's sister, the elderly Miss Thomasin Darling, who lived in the Wynding and acted as cook and general housekeeper to the visiting family. Miss Thomasin had a hare-lip and wore a formidable ginger-coloured cap. She was the soul of kindness, though, made excellent meals and was happily tolerant of sand (even when attached to sand-eels dug up by the children and brought home for the pot). A delicious supper of herring in a warm dining-room that smelt of mice, the sound of sea and wind – all this would send Mary and Emmie up the shallow stairs to their attic bedroom in a state of supreme contentment.

Their father too was content, back in his beloved North Country. In a very real sense this place became home to them all during those nomad years, when on their return from abroad they would have to find temporary perches with relatives or in lodgings. Except for people of the Crossleys' standing, most middle-class families rented their accommodation in the 19th century; there was nothing like today's fixation on house ownership. But there was a big difference between the lodgings the Bairds took in Lowestoft, for instance, one stormy and uncomfortable winter, and the family house they finally rented on a long lease in Teddington. Bamburgh, meanwhile, had become the one constant in their lives. Abroad, like the winters at home, always meant moving from place to place. Only

Bamburgh was the same: the old creaky house, the castle sprawled like a lion on its huge basalt rock, the ancient church with the wind buffeting its fortress tower.

After the family had settled in to Wynding House, John Forster Baird would be off to the Cheviots for grouse shooting or to Alnwick to visit his uncle, William. In Bamburgh he would hobnob with other visitors. Two of these were Alfred Hunt and his wife: he an ex-academic turned painter, she a woman whose wealth had enabled her husband to devote himself full-time to art. Did John Forster Baird envy him? They went out sketching together. Alfred Hunt exhibited at the Royal Academy and his pictures are now in the national collection (at Tate Britain). It is interesting to compare his works with those of John Forster Baird. Both men were landscape artists. Hunt's art is strikingly expressive, with strong colours and dramatic themes which would have been very much in tune with contemporary taste. John Forster Baird's, by contrast, is the work of a man who likes to capture a scene with the minimum of brushstrokes and imply rather than amplify its detail. But if the latter increasingly preferred the sketch to the full-blown painting and could not (or would not) 'nail his pictures to the wall', it was not something that disturbed his relationship with his more successful friend.

For the children Bamburgh was pure enjoyment. They swam, which their father insisted on. Even Auntie Jane, in a strange garb that looked like a serge pillowcase knotted at the ankles, bathed, though their mother did not. The children were allowed to take the hoops out of their home-made crinolines to caper about the sandhills and the beach, and tied up their skirts so they could hunt for crabs and winkles in the rock pools.

As the years passed a new diversion was found, play-writing and acting. Gertrude, now approaching her early teens, discovered a talent for drama. She would write holiday plays, to be read and rehearsed by the sisters on the beach, then acted in the Wynding in the evening. Mary would invariably be cast as the mother or the nurse; the current baby would be 'baby', and the others variously hero, heroine and villain.

The plays were historical dramas, inspired by tales of Forster glory and treachery. There was romance tucked into that family history of bad luck and bad judgement. Dorothy, the sister of the luckless Tom Forster who had fought on the Jacobite side in 1715 then been captured and imprisoned in Newgate, dressed up as a man and rode pillion behind a local blacksmith all the way to London to rescue her brother from certain execution and help him to safe exile in France. The Civil War and Stuart rebellions, events that have largely dropped out of public consciousness today, figured much in the imaginations of those Baird girls. 'Nasty little Roundhead,' a term of nursery abuse, showed which side the sympathies of that conservative family lay.

As the children grew up the need for a permanent base was becoming more urgent. John Forster Baird did not like the Thames valley, but he had friends in Teddington and the area was still semi-rural, with plenty of scope for exercise in the nearby parks and on the river; and it was not far from London and the Wimbledon rifle range. So the lease of Woodlands in Hampton Road (the postal address was 'Woodlands, Teddington') was secured. In 1870 the family moved there.

By then Mary was rising 15. She was mature for her age, gaining confidence in herself and the aptitudes she had acquired outside the schoolroom. She had a remarkable skill with the young, a normal enough ability in a large family but one she got particular satisfaction from; and two years later she would turn her experience to good use when she started teaching in the local Sunday school. She had also, in her role as head of the nursery, developed a strong sense of responsibility towards her siblings. The butterfly had not quite emerged from its chrysalis; when it did she would be all these things, plus one more as well – a focus for the admiration, not to say adoration, of the opposite sex. We can see this transition in her 1872 diary; and this is where Mary's story – as told by 16-year-old Mary – really begins.

Her journal opens with a ritual obeisance: 'I am afraid for the state of my soul. I fear I have not improved as much as I might . . . particularly in learning to control my own sorry and sinful, not to mention silly, thoughts, wishes and desires.' The family is yet again abroad. It is a rainy October day, they are staying in a mountainside chalet at Glion, near Montreux, in Switzerland:

I am writing in the large, comfortable Salon of the chalet, in the same room as Emmie, practising on the dreadful piano which appears used up by the weekly Church and Evangelical services. Thilda is reading an English book and the two little ones [Lilian and Evelyn] playing with a small friend of theirs, Geraldine Prettyman, the only child of a sweet-looking English lady in the chalet who is, at this moment, discussing with Mama children's ailments and (I suppose) 'little strangers'. Papa is drawing in the bedroom, and Gertrude beside him.

In these three sentences we can see how the family's English lifestyle travelled with them. You held services in your hotel on Sunday if you couldn't get to the nearest church, and there were plenty of other guests to fraternize with to take the place of the social life you had left at home. In this instance Emily-mother, pregnant again, was taking the sweet-faced (aptly named) Mrs Prettyman into her confidence. Later on Mary describes the people they met at the hotel's table d'hôte and the irreverent nicknames she and Gertrude had invented for them: 'Venus and Adonis' for a mother and son, 'Newgate' for a lugubrious man. But they were hemmed in by the rain which put them all in a bad mood ('if it goes on we shall "chrysalide" tomorrow into our spotted combies'). A few days later Mary had to reprove Gertrude for being impertinent. We don't know what form her impertinence took except that it was directed at their mother. Mary slipped from shared naughtiness at the dinner table into the role of disciplinarian with no difficulty. She was at the cusp, on the brink of adulthood, almost experimenting with it, you feel. Thilda persuaded her to join a dance in the hall of the hotel, but Mary was not happy: 'All the gentlemen had such sticky warm "fruzzy" hands that I went in gloves', and the strains of the 'Blue Danube' only made her nostalgic for 'a good spin with the best dancer in Teddington' (we shall come to him later). She dreaded the time when she would be expected to sing; this would happen when she was 18, but 'being not out, I am not often asked'.

Two days later the weather cleared. The family reverted to their walking routine down the mountain to Montreux for shopping, back by the same zigzag route ('my legs began to fail me . . . my face grew scarlet'). Mary felt she was the lazy one of the family and was slightly put out by Emmie 'the heedless', as she calls her, who at 18 months younger than her could outwalk the rest of them. The children were polarizing each other, Mary being pushed into questioning adulthood, Emmie cultivating an uncomplaining strength and biddableness and Gertrude turning more and more to her inner life of writing and drawing. But the sisters still played together. There was a nice moment on a later return journey in France when they all, teenagers and little ones as well, slept in a huge bed and had a pillow fight.

With her 17th birthday only two months away, Mary found the 'desire of living a new life burns strong again'. By this she meant a new deal with God, a commitment to lead a new life, 'in charity with all men, above all with Mama'. Mama was the problem, her 'ceaseless crossness', her 'incessant . . . fault-finding with me'. Mary cites incidents, like the catty remarks her mother made about the way she did her hair, and criticism of her in front of Emmie ('only her Papa and I know how bad Mary is') which make one seethe with indignation on her behalf. But Emily Baird was in the early months of pregnancy and probably feeling far from well, perforce left out of the major expeditions her husband organized and marginalized at a more profound level too by the attentions of Mary's first serious admirer, a certain Baron Niklaus von Baginsky.

Baginsky was staying in Glion. He haunted them throughout their time in Switzerland, pressing bouquets of flowers on Mary and seizing her hand whenever possible. We know nothing about him except that he was German and eccentric, and evidently totally smitten. Mary at first regarded him as a joke, then an irritating bore: 'the fact is the man never takes his eyes off me; it certainly makes me uncomfortable'. She found it hard to believe that it was her he was keen on, rather than the whole family acting as an attraction to a lonely man; but Thilda, whom she discussed this with, recognized the symptoms. Her parents did their best to protect her, her mother by treating him coolly and her father by showing 'a face of wrath'. But they also took the intrusive Baron with them on expeditions and he was there, at the foot of the Col de Jaman, resting on a mossy bank with Mary and her mother while the others climbed to the top. Her parents were clearly ambivalent, perhaps a little flattered on her behalf – so long as she was not serious. It was when she herself got involved with admirers later on that battle lines hardened.

Matters came to a head one day in late October. The family had gone on a nine-mile expedition to the Gorges du Trient, their father, Emmie, Gertrude and Lilian walking, Mary and her mother driving. On the return journey the party again divided, with Mary, Lilian and their father taking the train and the rest driving. Waiting at the station in St Maurice, who should they see jumping out of the Vevey train but the Baron.

He flew to us, shook hands with Papa, and then stuck out his hand to me. I had an idea he wished to shake hands, but as Mama has warned me against doing so with any stranger, I pretended to think he wished to borrow a pencil I held and pushed it into his hand, to his great disgust.

'*Nein, gaben Sie mir doch die Hand*' ['No, give me your hand'] said he, but I would not stand such impudent persistence, [and] rolled my hand more tightly in the fold of my cloak.

The Baron finally rushed off to catch his train – which he missed, to the great amusement of the girls as their train steamed out and they saw him sitting on the platform facing a two-hour wait. 'Papa's comment,' Mary notes, 'was characteristic. "Well, why didn't you shake hands with him?"'

Now the Baron had been seen off, John Forster Baird could afford to be generous.

In Paris, on their return journey, Mary had her photograph taken in the Rue de Rivoli. This is the face (see front cover) that so ensnared the Baron. But that womanly exterior concealed a teenager who two weeks earlier had written a list of the 'happiest moments in my life' which might have surprised the amorous Baron. They were:

Lilian's birth. Evelyn's birth. Uncle William's school treat at Stepney. Coming back from abroad to England. Sundays and Christmases at Teddington. My Confirmation, First Communion and subsequent Communions. My Sunday School hours, with Infants and Girls. (In a different way) parties at Teddington. Hours spent on the river (not really such fun and unmixed happiness as the punting). Days and hours and minutes with Savile at S [omerleyton]. Days spent with Mrs Oliver [a Northumbrian friend] and the baby. Every night after saying my prayers.

Her sorrows, she added, were being forbidden to go to Sunday school (one of her mother's punishments) and 'parting from Mrs Oliver'.

Home, babies, church, fun (particularly with the safe cousin-cum-best friend Savile) – these were Mary's props, the emotional scaffolding that supported her. In this list the Sunday school hours are the interesting item. She was not yet 17, but she had the confidence to manage a dozen children whom her sister Emmie, when she once took the class for her later on, found unmanageable. Mary loved teaching. If ever she was banned from these lessons she felt hugely deprived.

On the way home in October the family stopped in Paris for two nights. As they drove through the town by carriage they passed war-scarred buildings. It was 18 months since the establishment of the Paris Commune, the communist revolution and the civil war; two years since the Franco–Prussian War, when the Prussian army had besieged Paris and starved it into submission. Prussian militarism was changing the face of Europe. (Four years earlier, when the Bairds were researching their guide to the Tyrol, Austria had been defeated by its powerful neighbour at the battle of Sadowa.)

Mary was shocked by the devastation: 'trees riddled and barked with shot and shell, entire houses destroyed.' Karl Marx, writing shortly before this, saw beyond the pockmarked city to 'the dawn of the great social revolution which will forever free the human race from class rule. . . . Wonderful, indeed, was the change the Commune had wrought in Paris.' But to Mary this first sight of the effects of civil war – 'the destruction of their magnificent palaces by *themselves*!' – was very disturbing. The best part of their Paris visit for her was the afternoon they spent in the Louvre. A painting of the Virgin and Child by the 17th-century artist Giovanni Sassoferato particularly struck her, the infant 'a picture of baby plumpness and comfort, sleeping with clasped hands and half opened lips, like I have so often seen Evelyn'. (Evelyn in fact had slept on her arm the previous night in their shared bed at the hotel, which had helped to calm Mary after a fit of crying while she was undressing: 'I was thoroughly done up with hunger and excitement . . . as I generally am at the end of a journey.')

All in all the holiday had not been a great success for her. She hated changing homes so often and what she called 'fidgeting about always'. The weather had not helped, either ('a wet Sunday in dear England is disagreeable; here [Switzerland] it is simply intolerable'). There had been many moments of pleasure: the rediscovering of old friends from previous Swiss journeys, the beauty of the scenery, the fun of lunching in the mountains on 'walnuts and fresh air'; and even the hide-and-seek of the Baginsky episode was something to laugh about afterwards. But real life, she knew, was happening somewhere else, and that somewhere was Teddington. She revelled in the prospect of 'resettling in our delightful little abode', the (not so little) Woodlands. But here the word 'little' implied everything that creaky Swiss chalets, draughty foreign railway stations and large Paris hotels were not; that is to say, home.

7   *Jerry*

I cannot but think it must be a wrong sort of happiness.
Mary Baird, diary entry, February 11th 1874

The sound of the 'Blue Danube' in Glion had made Mary long for 'a good spin with the best dancer in Teddington'. Now that her 18th year was approaching and the milestone of 'coming out' in view, the world was suddenly full of new possibilities; and the best dancer in Teddington was waiting.

Jerry Burchell was the son of parents who might have stepped out of the pages of a Brönte novel – a wheelchair-bound father and a mad mother. What kind of madness she suffered from we do not know, but at least she wasn't locked in an attic. Times had changed, and the Burchells were a loving family. They lived in Park House, a large Georgian mansion opposite Bushey Park, a short walk away from the Bairds. There were three children: a son, Jerry, who was studying law, and two daughters, Edith and Amicia, about the same age as the elder Baird girls. The Burchells were very much part of the local church scene, but Mrs Burchell's illness occasioned frequent London visits (to see a specialist, or consign her to Bedlam? We do not know). So what with the Bairds' long summer holidays and visits to Somerleyton and the Burchells' trips to London, whenever he and they were in Teddington Jerry, already drawn to Mary by her looks, haunted the Baird house and sought every opportunity to coincide with her on the church circuit, to the considerable neglect of his legal studies. One can imagine the warmth and chatter of the Baird menage easily luring the young man away from his worrying home life. It was Mary, though, with her fascinating mix of piety and flirtatiousness, who soon became the main attraction.

We do not know what he looked like. How one wishes Mary had described him, but she was too attracted by him to notice what the component parts of this attractiveness were; as she says at one point, relaying a conversation between them, it is the way words are expressed that is everything. He was a devoted son: we see him through Mary's eyes at parties, bending over his father's chair, showing 'extreme attention to his father's every wish, expressed or unexpressed', while prayers for his mother, about whom he confided his anxieties to Mary, became a regular feature of their church-going.

After the family's return to Teddington in the autumn of 1872 there was a pause in the diary record, and no doubt in Jerry's attentions too, as over Christmas all three elder daughters got ill with fever, Emmie seriously. Typhoid was diagnosed, and when Emmie was well enough she was sent away (with shorn hair) to Somerleyton where she stayed for months, missing the birth of the new baby. Mary, meanwhile, became almost wholly responsible for preparing the baby's layette, making 'six nightgowns, . . . four pairs of minute socks, some small headsquares, flannel embroidered in scallops with buttonhole stitch'. She had 'left the schoolroom', and was appointed teacher to the six-year-old Evelyn (whom she found 'astonishingly dense' at additions and subtractions). She had also started her Sunday school teaching again which she was enjoying more than ever: 'All my "naughty" children moved up at Christmas, so I have a nice new lot to make friends with. . . . They bring me warm bouquets every Sunday—more scented than Baginsky's.'

She had remade Jerry's acquaintance at a local theatricals party soon after their return, a party that had ended in a dance, with the 'Blue Danube' and this handsome young neighbour as partner. But after their Christmas illnesses, the excitement over the expected baby left little spare time or emotion for flirting. From mid-March onwards she was living 'in daily expectation of the promised "little stranger"' (nicknamed 'Lancelot' in the vain hope it would be a boy). The baby in fact did not arrive till May 19th, which suggests either that parents and doctors only had the vaguest idea when it was due or, more likely, that there was so much reserve on the subject their mother kept even the older children in the dark. In the end when the day came, everybody's help was needed.

'Mama' popped her head round the schoolroom door where Mary was teaching Evelyn, telling her to hurry and fetch the doctor, their father having already gone to Isleworth for the nurse. Mary describes how she and Evelyn 'posted off' to Hampton to leave a note for the doctor, then 'scuttled off' to the surgery in Teddington to leave a message for him there, telegraphing Aunt Frank (Crossley) on the way. All that posting and scuttling, on foot, kept the family busy while the mother was in labour. By nine in the evening Mary could write triumphantly: 'Half a dozen daughters we are now! A baby girl is born. I have not seen her yet, but she arrived at 8 o'clock and has been screaming ever since.'

After the birth Mary's child-minding skills were, as ever, needed by her mother, and Mary was more than happy to cooperate. 'A sweeter specimen of babyhood I have never seen,' she notes, 'her qualities are too numerous to mention.' But as the blue-eyed baby lay kicking her legs in her bassinette, Mary's thoughts slid over to Jerry. He had not left off 'preferring' her, she said, and she was finding this preference difficult to resist. In a revealing phrase she writes: 'I wish, somehow, I were not so partial to Jerry, but what can I do when I see the way he looks at me.' Jerry set the pace; Mary was drawn along by it.

But in the process she was getting to know herself: 'I fear I am an awful flirt,' she says disingenuously. She could already look back on a succession of young men who had joined her in innocent hunt-the-lover games. Last year it had been her neighbour Freddy Johnson, followed by a young man she refers to as 'the inflammable Mortimer'; then the year before that there had been flirtatious late-night assignations with young Savile at Somerleyton. Baginsky, the most recent admirer, had somehow raised the stakes; this was the first time her eligibility had become a public matter, openly recognized by her parents. It was no coincidence that she fell seriously in love for the first time after this. Her natural state anyway was to be for ever on the edge of romance. The daily goings on of the family which her diary records – visitors, expeditions, holidays – may have the fascination of another world for us, but for her they could mean constriction and boredom. The only things she could really call her own were her Sunday school teaching and her love affairs. And for the first time these two private worlds of hers came together in her relationship with Jerry.

The two of them got on well 'in all serious matters', she wrote. This was brought home to her one morning when he quietly joined her during Communion. 'I can never quite forget . . . when I, being alone at the early Celebration became aware of him kneeling at my side before the altar rails! Was it an accident?'

This sense of fate, of their being destined to love each other, was very beguiling. And the circumstances of their lives played into their hands. It was only too easy for them to meet, walking as they frequently did between the two Anglican churches, St

Mary's down by the river and the newly built St Peter and Paul (the latter complete but for its spire, for which the girls collected money when they stayed at Somerleyton), at the nearer end of the town. It was in the newer church, where the ritual was more 'advanced' after its adoption of High Church practices, that Mary held her Sunday school classes. The incumbent vicar, Daniel Trinder, had raised hackles when he had first introduced the new rituals which included incense and coloured vestments and turning east for the creed. There were stories of cabbages being thrown and angry parishioners turning west instead of east. But by the time the Bairds arrived these divisions were becoming blurred. The aesthetic luxuriousness of the new rituals must have seemed appropriate in this pretty suburb; after all, the railway (which had arrived in 1863) had brought other well-off families beside the Bairds and the Burchells to the neighbourhood. Teddington's wealth mirrored the increasing affluence of the nation. And prosperity encouraged tolerance. The Baird and Trinder families became good friends, one-time nonconformist Emily gladly dispensing cups of tea to the high-church Mr Trinder and his brood. (Interestingly, William Baird, John Forster Baird's brother, whose school treat at Stepney had been on Mary's list of favourite things, had recently published a sermon advocating a burying of hatchets between the Methodists and the Church of England. Reconciliation was in the air.)

Church – several times during the week, three times on Sundays – provided the perfect cover for Mary and Jerry; and all this meeting at services and walking home together (albeit with other members of the family, though younger sisters could easily be shaken off) was forcing the pace. By August they had exchanged photographs and, according to Mary, 'done many other foolish things'. A few months earlier Mary had made a trip to London to stay with Aunt Frank and go to the theatre during her cousin Savile's half-term. This had revived fond memories of the fun and games of two years earlier when 'Savile and I lived in each other's solicitude'. Jerry's hold on her heart faltered during one giddy week of musical comedies and ballet, and when the two cousins enjoyed an evening walk from St John's Wood to the Langham Hotel, where the party was staying, the comment this evokes from Mary tells one a lot about the ease of this affectionate cousinship, in contrast to the tensions of serious courting: 'A pleasant walk home, *laughed* with SBC [Savile] in the moonlight' (Mary's emphasis).

Back in Teddington, however, she decided 'there is such a thing as having too many strings to one's bow'. As she and Jerry approached a summer of separation when he would be in London, the Bairds in Northumberland, Jerry appeared to seal his claim by the manner of his farewell: 'He laid down his two hands on my own, and pressing them, looked into my eyes with that peculiar expression with which no one ever looked at me before.' In theory a suitor still had to approach the parents first before making a declaration of his love. But John Forster Baird was visibly hostile, Emily uneasy. Ironically this gave a kind of licence to the young couple when they realized a formal approach might well be baulked. Enforced secrecy might mean constraint, but also a kind of freedom to make your own rules within it.

During the family's two-month stay in the north ('our northern banishment,' Mary calls it: Bamburgh had suddenly lost its charm) they corresponded through Jerry's sister, Edith, exchanging copied hymns and books. But Mary was not well; the emotional strain was taking its toll. The family had had a gruelling journey. It began badly when a drunken cabby crashed the springs of his horse-drawn cab on Waterloo Bridge, which meant unloading all of the luggage and nearly missing the train at King's Cross. At York Mary felt faint (she had had no breakfast) and had 'mild hysterics', a phrase that occurs several times in her diaries (Gertrude has mild hysterics before her confirmation, Mary again when her father finally agrees to a two-year engagement). Were such hysterics just a sudden of rush of emotion or fatigue that anybody might have which could bring on tears, or something more dramatic? Whatever she did – snivelled, wept or raged – Mary was 'blown up thoroughly' by her mother. And when, a few days later, she fainted in church she was sent to the Bamburgh doctor who diagnosed 'poverty of blood'. 'Strong steel', medicinal iron, was prescribed. Though bad for the teeth, 'steel' was a standard remedy for many teenage ills and, in this case, seems to have had the desired effect. Mary was soon bathing every day, and she describes a delightful expedition to Dunstanburgh with her father and a family staying in Bamburgh Castle, the Newalls, who had teenage sons. She and the boys 'ran around all over the ruins and rocks, and had great fun raising an echo with all the power of our voices and imitating the bleating of sheep'. This is the other Mary, perhaps not quite ready yet to 'begin life in good earnest', a phrase she uses of the Newalls' sister, a Mrs Cookson, a newly wed in 'a soft falling green dress with gold ornaments' who looks 'so very young' – too young, the implication is, to embark on this next serious phase of life. Somewhere at the back of Mary's mind must have been the thought that married women do not run around among ruins pretending to be sheep.

On one level, John Forster Baird's opposition to the Jerry match seems perfectly understandable. Jerry was without qualifications (did he have a private income?) and less than dedicated to his studies. But as in the Baginsky episode, one senses something a little less than rational in her father's opposition. We are in primeval territory here, Rapunzel country, though both father and daughter can happily slip back into the playful routines of earlier times, as the Dunstanburgh episode illustrates. As in all families, these changes of mood and the nuances that go with them create endless fluctuation of colour and tone which each entry in Mary's diary captures graphically. With the benefit of hindsight, we can see how Mary's personality was developing, and the way her life was heading. John Forster Baird, however, could not. All he could see was a wayward daughter whose face was her fortune (virtually her only one, given the size of his family and the way they lived), who needed protection both from suitors, present and future, and, perhaps equally importantly, from her own flirtatious self.

But once they were back in Teddington things began to move fast. By mid-December, in the week following Mary's 18th birthday, Jerry had declared himself. Mary was ecstatic: 'It is out at last! Jerry and I each know what our feelings are with regard to each other!' She reported their conversation in dialogue form.

He asked me, 'How long have you liked me?'

'How long have you liked me?'

He said, 'You remember the Wilbrahams' croquet party [July 3rd 1872]? When I saw you there, I thought you were the sweetest girl I ever saw; and your own party [February 4th 1873] quite finished it up!'

Then I said, 'Suppose you saw somebody else you liked better? . . .'

The loving look came into his eyes, as he said, 'My darling, is it likely?'

Then we promised to stick together, and above all pray together for the accomplishment of our wish.

Her mother surprised this little tête-à-tête. She looked astonished, and blushed 'as if she were twenty', Mary writes. The three of them then went, amicably enough, back to Woodlands; and 'while Mama was laying down her hat, Jerry put his arm around my waist, and drew me up close to him; whereupon I thinking that not yet allowable, quietly disengaged myself, and he contented himself with softly stroking my hand, and looking at me as if he would like "to eat me up", for that is the only term which seems to express his looks.' The three of them met again at church that evening. Jerry walked home with them, 'only we could not say anything but squeeze'.

Mary's vivid prose captures the emotion of the day. A fraught winter lay ahead of her. High minded plans for beginning her 19th year by 'partaking of the Holy Eucharist' at early service the following Sunday are interrupted by the words 'Jerry said – '. Then a page is torn out. 'My times are in Thy Hand!' she concludes. The exclamation mark suggests she knew they might be stormy.

Jerry sought an interview with her father. It was refused. John Forster Baird was implacable. Through her mother the message came back that, reasonably enough, Jerry should first pass his law exams before any understanding between the young couple could even be considered. Meanwhile, Jerry was not to come to the house – to the lovers' consternation: 'Jerry was dreadfully dismayed, and I howled, but the next day we had a walk in the park, and settled that no opposition would interfere with our love to each other.' Mary took to defiance with zeal. When, soon afterwards, the first kisses were exchanged she can see no harm, and notes with glee that 'Mama' has not been informed.

But the parents had ancient weapons on their side. Mary and Emmie were whisked off by their father to a ball at Moor Hall, the house near Kidderminster of uncle John Brinton. (Mary commented: 'A hundred people, and more were there, among them heaps of cousins of whom I can write nothing very pleasant.') Then came a two-week stay at Somerleyton ('this dreadful place', she called it), the company including 'a Dissenting minister as ugly as sin'. Mary was thoroughly jaundiced by now. There was a brief moment of fun on the return train journey with Savile and his tutor, A.L. Smith, a Fellow of Trinity College Oxford, who had been one of the Somerleyton party, and the latter's dog Gudrun (good-run). The three of them made a dummy out of their coats so the compartment looked full; and the trip ended with an even greater moment of fun when Jerry (in defiance of the rules?) met them at Waterloo Station.

We can imagine her father's reaction; and as we watch him at Waterloo, about to shepherd his family on to the homeward train while he takes himself off to town, there is another factor to consider. John Forster Baird was by now a member of the Garrick Club. There he met lawyers, writers, artists and actors who were the cream of London society. He had virtually given up his conveyancing but he still registered himself as barrister-at-law, and he would surely have kept quiet about his painting in a club that included John Everett Millais among its members. Here at the Garrick he again could have bumped into Henry Irving, who had been blackballed when he first applied, but was now one of the club's most famous members. But whoever he met, all this brushing shoulders with the rich and famous must have made John Forster Baird more dubious than ever at the prospect of his eldest daughter tying herself up with a suburban lawyer of complicated family background. Membership of the Garrick would also have helped refurbish his own self-image as he chatted to fellow members across that convivial dining-room table. One of the club's habitués he certainly would have introduced himself to was the friendly Anthony Trollope – after all, he had known his brother Tom in Florence. And a subject he and Trollope might well have discussed, given John Forster Baird's preoccupation with his children's future and its topicality (the first Education Act had been passed in 1870) was education.

The Trollope family had employed a French governess who now ran a school in Hove, reputed to have high academic standards, where Anthony's niece, Bice, had gone. It was useful to know this – that Madame Collinet, as she was called, ran a respectable school for young ladies at Albany Villas, Hove, on the healthy south coast within a short walk of the sea.

Meanwhile, in the aftermath of the girls' visit to the Brinton clan, and fortified perhaps by good advice from her sisters, Emily engineered a useful compromise. If all idea of an engagement was dropped, Jerry could visit the house like any normal visitor. It was a curious arrangement, in effect a kind of fiction: if the young couple gave up all idea of being serious, they could go on seeing each other. But of course, they would not give it up. Thus by the time of Mary's coming-out ball on Tuesday January 27th 1874, nearly two months after her 18th birthday, when she, Thilda, her father and her mother (sitting on her husband's lap) arrived in their hired carriage at the Griffen Hotel in Kingston, Jerry was waiting, and he immediately asked Mary for a dance ('he pounced on me'). First, though, she had to parade round the room and up to the dais where local dignitaries were seated. She was wearing white muslin, 'a long skirt trimmed with deep flounces behind', crystal drops on a black choker and white flowers in her hair. Among the many delightful things Jerry told her as they danced ('which I cannot write') was a compliment he had overheard – that Mary 'quite cut out anybody else in the room'. John Forster Baird thus had the mixed satisfaction of seeing his daughter the belle of the ball and all eyes on her as she waltzed with the unsuitable Jerry. He must have realized it was only a matter of time before he would lose her. The question was, to whom? Only two days earlier, on a Sunday which, like all Woodlands Sundays, was full of church and unexpected guests, Jerry had turned up for tea,

Jerry

coinciding with A.L. Smith who had '*walked*' from Kensington (Mary's emphasis: it was all of 12 miles). Why had A.L. Smith turned up? Nobody appeared to wonder; he was an old family friend, and everyone was busy with the evening hymn-singing. Much more important for Mary was the fact that she and Jerry had 'a nice affectionate conversation in the corner by the piano'. In the glow of her flirtation, Mary must have looked a changed person from the depressed girl she had been at Somerleyton. Her father, meanwhile, infuriated that he was unable to put a stop to the affair and dismayed to discover that Jerry was there when he came in at the end of the afternoon, was biting his lip – and hoping that Jerry would flunk his law exams.

He did fail them the following summer; hardly surprisingly, given how much of his time he had been spending with Mary. But before that her diary stops. She concludes with a characteristic confession ('I am not half as attentive in Church as I was. . . . I lie too long in bed in the morning') and asks, 'How can I be so happy when I am so wicked. . . . I cannot think but that it must be a wrong sort of happiness? – and yet that cannot be . . . when I think of the many blessings God has given me; everything I once wished and prayed for – a new baby, permission to teach in Sunday school, to go daily to Evensong . . . and to crown it all a lover who can help in my religious difficulties, a friend in fact.' She ends the diary with a sigh of satisfaction and a prayer that God may bring her and Jerry through the troubles that may beset them.

At the end of March the 17-year-old Emmie takes over the story. There is no deliberate sequence here, it is just accident that her diary follows Mary's, and our luck. Immediately, with Emmie, we are on a different planet. Their handwriting tells you the difference – Mary's is spiky and rapid, often illegible, Emmie's rounder, easier to read. If her mother is the go-between between Mary and her father (often getting caught in crossfire), Emmie is the bridge between mother and eldest daughter; and our bridge to Gertrude. These two younger sisters were much closer to each other than either was to Mary, as if the latter's intense personality necessitated some sort of defensive alliance between her immediate siblings. Emmie uses her diary, like Mary, to express her secret thoughts, but they differ from Mary's in two profound respects: she does not pour her emotion into religion (though, a true daughter of her age, she is of course concerned with the state of her soul), and she is no flirt.

In the very first entry, Mary's room is differentiated from the rest of the house as having 'an odour of sanctity like a Roman Catholic church', this after Jerry had given them some incense. Emmie was worried that she would not be able to keep the resolutions she wrote on her Resolution Card offered up in church at the end of a visiting mission by a certain Mr Ridgeway, who was infinitely more sympathetic to her than the intellectual Mr Trinder. 'I must remember what he said about not despairing, and renewing a resolution again and again.' Emmie, you realize, has an inbuilt low self-esteem. Mary may beat her breast at her own spiritual unworthiness but the next minute she is off on the track of the current love affair. Emmie knows she is not ready for that sort of thing – maybe she never will be. She is shy: 'I do dislike parties, and society in general, sometimes. . . . Oh dear, I am sure I am meant to be an old maid! I never liked anybody yet in *that* way', and she adds she almost envies Mary, it seems to make her happier. 'It,' though, is something that happens to other people, not to her.

Emmie's diary lasts from March 25th 1874 till the end of the year. She wants to make it a record of their family life and, like Mary, begins by setting the scene: 'It is a lovely evening for

March. I am sitting in the schoolroom writing, Gertrude is doing confirmation questions upstairs, Thilda is singing; we have just . . . returned from the Richmond drawing class.' The girls' chat is all about the approaching confirmations (Gertrude's and Thilda's, the latter converting to Anglicanism from German Lutheranism) and the relative merits of the different preachers; then the next evening, after an afternoon see-sawing in the Trinders' garden, comes another scene-set: 'We are all sitting in the schoolroom, Mary reading with her elbows on the arm-chair, Gertrude writing, Thilda sewing, the children playing. It is so nice and comfortable-looking I might just as well stop and write a bit. Jerry has been here lately, on the whole.' That is very Emmie – a short phrase qualifying what she has just said, as if she doubts her own observations. I have two photographs of her; in each she has a shy, self-effacing look. She grew up to be very elegant, with a Gainsborough-like beauty, but never lost that look of gentle uncertainty. Her diary has none of Mary's tartness. But we get a new slant on the Jerry–Mary relationship. And we see, quite early on, that things are not going smoothly.

'I *should* not like my lover to say my movements were "like those of an old cow," but'– doubting Emmie again – 'I suppose it is his [Jerry's] way.' Emmie and Gertrude decide Mary will get as good as she gives ('she has quite enough of her own way at home'). But the 'old cow' remark rankles with all of them and is compounded later when Jerry criticizes Mary's – and all the girls' – new hats of 'fine blue felt . . . with broad brims and round tops . . . and a light blue feather'. He says they are hideous, at which the children gang up on him and tell Mary he has no taste ('Not *my* idea of a lover,' Emmie says loyally, 'he ought to think everything *she* wears perfect!')

Emmie's idealistic picture of how a lover should behave was going to be revised. But in the intervening period, during the spring of 1874, Mary and Jerry had been very lover-like, never missing an opportunity to walk together or sit next to each other on joint outings or at evening parties. There was the Boat Race, the Henley Regatta, walks in the park and endless meetings in the Baird home ('Jerry to dinner, tea and supper') – all the occasion for a lot of fun for the elder girls as well as a chance for the young couple to 'spoon' (Emmie's disparaging term). On an April Saturday Emmie and her great friend Cecil Darnell, eldest daughter of the vicar of Bamburgh, who was staying with them, went with Mary and Jerry to Kew and had 'a regular rampage' (hide-and-seek?). Emmie, content in the companionship of her close friend, was happy to let Mary and Jerry sit apart and only catch up with the others after they had left the park. One gets glimpses in both these diaries of the loneliness that an individual can feel in the heart of a large family. These bosom friends – Jerry, in Mary's case, and Cecil, in Emmie's – allowed each girl to feel that they had a separate existence beyond the family scene.

The Darnells' visit (Cecil came with one of her sisters) was the occasion for some serious sight-seeing. John Forster Baird took them out two days running, first to Westminster and the City, then to the Crystal Palace. They took the train to Waterloo and on the first day walked to Westminster, saw Westminster Hall and Abbey and the Court of the Queen's Bench, then went by steamer to London Bridge, walked 'through the slums', Emmie reports, to Billingsgate and the Tower, which they visited; walked to St Paul's, climbed up to the Whispering Gallery and the Golden Gallery ('splendid view of the whole of London'); sat in on Evensong ('greatly rested!'), then walked back to Waterloo for the 5.20 Teddington train. The following day they 'did' Crystal Palace: 'the "antediluvian animals" . . . the "aborigines" . . . the Egyptian and Pompeian and Arts Courts

. . . the tropical end . . . the aquarium.' Not surprisingly Emmie was exhausted the next day and having written all this up went to bed early 'after behaving like a baby' (her words).

In the context of Victorian middle-class life such physical stamina is perhaps not surprising. Meals were regularly served up, household chores done by others. All those unseen servant hands created not merely time but energy for their employers. The Bairds took on a new maid ('our fourth servant') that summer; Emmie noted she was almost the same age as herself but 'ever so much smaller. . . . I shouldn't like to be her.' But servants were part of the fabric of life; and apart from this mention and one other, when the cook and nursery maid quarrel, they do not figure in the diaries. By the standards of some of the people the Baird parents mixed with, their household was probably quite modest. The latest maid was only acquired after a new and unexpected infusion of wealth.

On their return from the Crystal Palace, Auntie Jane was waiting for them. Poor Auntie Jane, ever associated with family crises, was this time the bringer of bad news. Uncle William Baird, John Forster Baird's uncle – of that earlier letter about drainage and the 'blind' pub – was ill, and Auntie Jane (of course) was about to set off to look after him. Mary evidently had scant use for her uncle, that 'poor, silly old man' as she'd called him in her Bamburgh diary, and she is invariably critical of her aunt too; but Emmie was more charitable: 'Auntie Jane can't help her natural, noisy manner.'

The children think no more of this. Everything, even the Mary–Jerry romance, is suddenly secondary to the great day when Gertrude and Thilda are to be confirmed by the bishop. But when the day comes the veiled candidates have to wait for nearly four hours before the bishop – or archdeacon, as he turns out to be – arrives; meanwhile the congregation sit out the long wait uncomplainingly as hymns, sermons and more hymns fill the gap, though several of the girls faint. (Such longueurs were evidently a common part of Victorian church life: a few weeks earlier Emmie, Mary and Jerry had taken a swig of brandy each to help them through the rigours of Easter Sunday, and Emmie at one point recorded a 44-minute sermon by Mr Trinder.)

More bad news, though, was on the way. While Auntie Jane was staying with him at his home at Windy Edge, great-uncle William Baird had shot himself following a bout of depression brought on by an unspecified terminal illness. John Forster Baird left immediately for the north. Surprisingly, the children did not put on mourning; a few days later Mary and Emmie were wearing their 'blue ticking frocks' and the younger girls white muslin. Was Uncle William not considered important enough for mourning? Important he certainly was, though, as the family were soon to find out. Their father returned to announce they would be £2,000 a year better off, at least that is what Emmie says. £200 a year (£10,000 today) would be a more realistic figure, but whichever it was, it was going to make a very significant improvement in the Baird finances. William Baird's estate was valued at under £25,000 (he had been the other major inheritor of the original William Baird's estate along with John Forster-surgeon and, good husbandman that he was, he had made his share prosper). His residuary legatee was John Forster Baird.

The first outward and visible sign of their new wealth that Emmie records is their father's moustache: he'd had it dyed by the Alnwick hairdresser ('It doesn't match the rest of him, I hope it will fade' is her comment); and true to form, he had bought another property, Thomson's Walls, near Bowmont Hill. The two elder girls might, they were told, get dress allowances of £40 each and a seal skin next winter, information which scared

Above left: John Baird, surgeon,
aged 37; *above right*: his wife Mary Baird, née Potts, aged 30. Watercolour portraits
by Edward Hastings, 1827.

Above left: John Forster Baird, aged 14; *above right*: Jane Baird, aged 11. Watercolour
portraits by Edward Hastings, 1837.

Above left: Anna Maria Baird, aged nine; *above right*: William Baird, aged one year. Watercolour portraits by Edward Hastings, 1837.

Bamburgh Castle, Northumberland; watercolour by John Forster Baird.

Above left: John Forster Baird, aged 52; *above right*: Emily Baird, aged 45.

Above right: Emmie Baird, aged 18; *above left*: Mary Baird, aged 20.

Gertrude Baird, aged 17 (*left*), and photographed after her death (*above*).

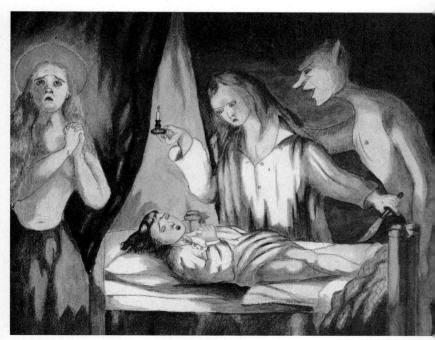

Untitled watercolour by Gertrude Baird, June 1873.

Untitled watercolour by Gertrude Baird, inscribed 'G.A.B. February 10 1874'.

Untitled watercolour by Gertrude Baird, circa 1874.

Above: Untitled watercolour, painted by Gertrude Baird in her mid-teens, circa 1874.

Left: Page of Mary Baird's coded diary, April 12th 1877.

Left: Arthur Lionel Smith, aged 9½, as a full-time boarder at Christ's Hospital, 1860.

Above left: Mary Baird in Paris, May 1877. This was a photograph that she disliked: 'I have got my mouth open, and am looking so ridiculously sentimental that I could not make up my mind to send the spare negative to C.A.G. [Charles Allix Griffith] as I intended.' *Above right*: Arthur Lionel Smith, aged 17, in the uniform of a Graecian at Christ's Hospital, 1868.

Above: In the gardens of Trinity College, Oxford, June 1877. Mary Baird is standing next to Lady Crossley ('Aunt Frank') in the back row, Savile Crossley sits astride the chair, Emmie Baird is sitting second from the right. A.L. Smith is at the front on the grass.

Left: Arthur Lionel Smith, aged 27, after becoming engaged to Mary Baird in 1877.

Gertrude, evidently the most prudent of the sisters ('Mama's new "rustic" seats for the garden, the refrigerator [sic] and croquet set seem a load upon her mind', says Emily). There was an interesting change in mood in the aftermath of Uncle William's death. The girls were more relaxed – because of their father's absence in the north? This certainly affected Mary and Jerry.

Emmie describes a conversation between her and Mary, one of those spontaneous moments when family bonds were reinforced, with the help of near-darkness and laughter. It was dusk, on Whit-Sunday evening (four days after the news of Uncle William's death), after a day when, with Mary safely at Sunday school, Emmie had talked in confidence to Jerry and 'he explained things I was puzzled about so well and clearly' – what things, she does not specify, but one can make guess.

We were very late going to bed, but I went into Mary's room, and talked to her, while she brushed her hair – we were talking 'the subject'. Mary said it felt so queer to feel a little girl still through it, sometimes. Suddenly the difference struck me too and I began to laugh. Mary has been so strange and different, 'grown-up' to me this last year – but last night when she had her hair down and was talking nicely, I could not help remembering how she and I used to be, and what a pretty little girl she was – oh, it seems so strange to think now all is so different, and those jolly old times will never come again!

Mary had been happy that weekend. Jerry had spent most of it with her, and the weather was perfect. But events were conspiring against the lovers. 'Papa is more against that affair than ever,' Emmie noted. Then, two weeks later, came the news that Jerry had failed his exams. He would take them again in the autumn, he said. But the young man was understandably stressed, and this did not bring out the best side of him. The usual summer dispersal took place: some of the Bairds abroad (father, Emmie and Lilian), the rest to Somerleyton, then all of them to north Wales where Emmie had a severe attack of pink-eye. Everybody was feeling worse for wear, in spite of the holiday. Mary looked pale and thin – 'it must all be that Jerry's fault,' Emmie decided. By November, with exams looming again, Jerry and Mary were quarrelling: he called her 'horrid', she cried, Jerry wrote apologizing ('it was all owing to his vile temper that he had lost her', he told Emmie), her father was still determined to 'smash' it. When Jerry did finally pass his exams John Forster Baird insisted on a two-year probation before any engagement.

There was much coming and going to and from Somerleyton during those months. One can imagine the attitude of the Crossley aunt, all sympathy with the love-lorn (and now confused) niece, behind-the-scenes support for her parents: family elders tend to play double games in these situations. John Forster Baird wrote to Jerry setting out his terms, a letter that was mysteriously opened by Jerry's father, who wrote back very reasonably saying that if the young couple knew their own minds, why shouldn't they get engaged. Relations between the two fathers temporarily cooled.

A war of attrition was being waged on Mary. Under this onslaught she began to doubt. (In a 'happy' family which does not quarrel it is sometimes difficult to muster one's defences.) All Mary's conditioning – her sense of duty, her instinctive love and loyalty to her father – was undermining her resolve; while her father's did not waver. We will never know what he disliked so much about the young man, but John Forster Baird's sheer force of personality, or his obduracy, left all three of the women in the story – Emily, Mary and Emmie – swivelling like weathercocks, one moment for it, the next against. Even Mary. She wanted to go away for a year, she said, the wear and tear was getting her down. She did escape, to Somerleyton of course, where she wrote to Jerry breaking it off, then got a streaming cold (everyone was ill that year) so could not return to Teddington till after Christmas.

But then there was a sudden calm. The affair was on again. Mary (under pressure from Somerleyton?) agreed to the two-year proposal, Jerry had a talk with John Forster Baird; the two had met, skating (it was a cold winter) on the Long Water at Hampton Court, and Jerry had been invited home to tea; 'Papa' (this is Emmie reporting her mother's words) 'behaved like an angel'. Why the sudden volte-face? Perhaps, aware of his influence over Mary, he decided to be lenient, knowing things would go his way in the end; as they did. Mary and Jerry did not marry, nor even become formally engaged. But the final unraveling happened outside the pages of any diary, so we have none of the details. But we can imagine them. The relentless opposition, broken by this sudden Pavlovian niceness, ensured that the couple were under maximum strain. Mary's exhaustion and Jerry's temper did the rest.

Emmie ends her diary with an evocative entry, the last of 1874:

My room, 10.30 pm. Doty is in bed. . . . Mary came back [from Somerleyton] at 6 pm, oh we were so glad to see her again! We have been doing nothing but skate lately. . . . Generally we are about 5 hours on the ice. – So the old year is passing away! Well, it has been a nice one! And has brought us much happiness, more than we deserve to balance the disagreeables. Mama has just come in to hurry me to bed, so I must be quick. My room is so cosy, with a nice fire. I want to hear the bells tonight, ringing the new year in – but I am tired. Oh! how happy we are. I wonder what the new year will bring us?

At the moment of writing, glowing from skating and the comforting fire, Emmie had forgotten much, not just the ups and downs of the Jerry affair but another little cloud hovering over the new year. She had mentioned it in an earlier entry: 'Mama says she thinks of sending my Dotina [Gertrude] to school, either at Brighton or Brussels. Perhaps 'tis only talk, but if she did go, I should miss her dreadfully.'

Education was something Emmie herself yearned for. When the opportunity for it did occur it offered itself to her sister, not to her; and it was not to turn out how she, or any of them, expected.

8   *Education*

Let all, both men and women, have equal chances of
maturing such intellect as God has given them.
Millicent Fawcett, 1868.

Without realising it, the Bairds were in the grip of a mood that
was sweeping Europe. Education reforms had been introduced,
or soon would be, in Prussia, Switzerland, Belgium, Italy and
the Netherlands, while in England the 1870 Education Act
followed inevitably on the Second Reform Act of three years
earlier, which had doubled the number of urban voters. Given
the huge school-less population of young people and the
pressure from industry for literate workers, it was generally
agreed that more education was needed. But the question was,
how much; and the fear – that too much might be dangerous –
inevitably meant that when the act was finally passed it was a
compromise. Universal elementary education was introduced,
but it would not be made compulsory for another ten years.

The aim of the act was 'to complete the present voluntary
system, to fill up gaps . . . not to destroy the existing system in
introducing a new one'. These cautious words were those of the
bill's proposer, William Forster MP. One can imagine John
Forster Baird's eye being caught by the name (William Forster

was a northerner too). The new schools in any case were for the masses, not for governess-reared products of the middle classes. But education was in the air, and the Bairds, whether they liked it or not, had caught the prevailing trend. Serious education for women would soon be part of that *zeitgeist* too.

With plans for Gertrude's schooling afoot, Emmie was left to ponder her own ignorance. 'I have begun to read Grecian and Roman history with energy, upon finding myself deficient in general knowledge, I only hope the fit won't wear off, and leave me idle as before.' She longed to be better educated, but the enormity of the task was daunting. When some fine weather came along and the French teacher was away she could not stop herself exclaiming: 'Happiness! no French tomorrow!' Self-improvement was not a straightforward task.

At a superficial level the Baird children were moderately well educated, certainly cultured. They spoke and wrote German with ease, French reasonably well, could play the piano and draw. They were also well read.

The diaries are full of references to reading aloud: French children's books, which their mother translated as she read, Victorian classics (a little less classic than they are today) and German novels. Reading aloud was a family ritual. Similar in some ways to television today, it provided a focus for family life and a relief from unexpected tensions, while acting as an informal educational tool for reinforcing family bonds and moral codes.

Emmie mentions her father reading Trollope aloud: *Barchester Towers*, which she preferred to *The Warden*. She had Mrs Gaskell's *Sylvia's Lovers* read to her by Mary when she had pink-eye (they both cried at the end – probably quite healthy for the pink-eye); then she herself read an unnamed German book aloud to her sisters and Thilda in Bushey Park; and Gertrude asks her father for Goethe's *Life*. But culture was not education. Emmie was still wracked by her sense of lack of knowledge: 'I do not know enough – everyday I feel my ignorance more.' She regretted the departure of the Darnells after their stay, but 'it will be nice after all settling down to hard work again, which is what we must do! We must work hard! and try to learn more!' This poignant phrase rang a bell for me; then I remembered the words of Sonia, another junior female trapped in a marginalized role, at the end of *Uncle Vanya*: 'Yes, yes, work. As soon as we've seen the others off, we'll settle down to work.' Chekhov's turn-of-the-century Russia was not so different a place from the world of the Bairds, though Sonia's work, with estate accounts, was nothing like Emmie's. But the latter might have recognized familiar elements in Sonia's oppression. In both societies duty to family – parents or husband – was considered sufficient object for female aspirations. Emmie's spirit instinctively longed for the freedom that education could bring. She felt despair when she stared her 'horrible ignorance' in the face.

She was on the brink of turning 18 and abandoning formal education for ever. Mary had been impatient to leave the schoolroom, but in Emmie the prospect induced near-panic: 'I am nearly eighteen, oh, misery, would I were younger!' Too late to learn any more, too late to be more than a wallflower at the side of a world she felt barely equipped for.

Society beyond Woodlands was changing. Gladstone's reforming first ministry had introduced elementary education, the reform of the civil service, a relaxing of restrictions on trade unions and (more important for the Crossley and Brinton clans, those who had not already gone over to Anglicanism) on dissenters. Even in a family as apolitical as the Bairds, the new mood in the country must have been felt, though the only time Emmie mentioned Gladstone's name was on their Welsh – pink-eye – holiday, when the girls stood in the crowd at the wedding of Gladstone's nephew (attended by Mrs G. but not the great man himself). Emmie's description of it gives no hint of Baird political leanings, nor Mary's curt comment that it was 'about as dismal as a funeral!' – this time, not one she enjoyed.

How the new provisions for education were going to affect women was clear: very little. When the act was passed there were only enough schools for half the number of school-aged children in the country; six years later that had risen to three-quarters. But in a situation where boys and girls would be in competition for school places, girls were unlikely to win. Overall, the sponsors of the act turned their back on any radical innovation, resisting pressure from groups such as the National Education League which was lobbying for universal and free compulsory education. The education debate had gone on with increasing intensity for over a decade, but the agenda had been firmly set by the Newcastle Commision, set up in 1858 to examine the state of elementary education. The Commission's conclusion was that universal compulsory education was 'neither attainable nor desirable.' Four years later Robert Lowe MP, Vice-President of the Committee of the Privy Council concerned with education, told Parliament: 'We do not profess to give these children an education that will raise them above their station or business in life,' rather 'to give them an education that may fit them for that business.' Existing social structures were not to be undermined.

The link between lack of education and civil unrest was recognized. William Forster MP spoke of the great good the government hoped would result 'by removing the ignorance which we are all aware is pregnant with crime and misery, with misfortune to individuals, and danger to the community. . . . Now that we have given them political power [in the Second

Reform Act of 1867] we must not wait any longer to give them education.' But when it came to education, 'them' was still no one over the age of 12; and it was certainly not young women

So what was an aspiring teenage girl to do? The women's cause had been taken up by radical intellectuals, among them Millicent Fawcett, quoted at the beginning of this chapter, who as editor of the *Englishwoman's Review* pressed for educational opportunities for women, as did her husband for extending the suffrage to them (a cause toyed with by Disraeli before the 1867 Act, on the grounds that 'in a country governed by a woman [Queen Victoria] . . . I do not see . . . on what reasons, if you come to right, she has not a right to vote'). By the early 1870s the Girls' Public Day School Trust had been founded. Mary was later to educate all her seven daughters at a GPDS school. The Cambridge Local Examinations had meanwhile been opened to girls, though not yet the university (later, three of Mary's daughters would go to Cambridge, do the exams but not get formal degrees). Local associations for women's higher education were mushrooming in the 1870s, and under their auspices a sort of proto-Open University system developed, with lectures in provincial centres given by Oxbridge graduates, intended for governesses and daughters at home. Already, by the mid-1870s, nearly a quarter of the candidates for the Cambridge local exams were women, and by then they had somewhere to go on to. Girton College had been founded in 1869 and the first Oxford women's colleges followed within ten years.

But all this was useless to Emmie. One possibility, earlier on, might have been Cheltenham Ladies' College, founded in the mid-1850s; and London, which had been at the forefront of the campaign for women's education, had Bedford College and its Working Women's Colleges in Queen's and Fitzroy Squares for further and higher education. There were opportunities, and any of these last three would have been accessible from Teddington. But Emmie was not a working woman, and it is doubtful whether her parents had heard of any of these places, even Cheltenham. The Bairds were too entrenched in the old system: daughters should be educated at home. Hence the succession of governesses, hence – because not all of them were sympathetic – Emmie's joy when French was cancelled.

But her sense of deprivation grew. She tried 'self-help' (Samuel Smiles' classic book of that name, about great men, had been published in 1859), but found it almost made matters worse. To start reading about the Greeks and the Romans only showed you how little you knew. Her mother, characteristically, added to her misery by laughing at her for asking who Colenso and the Pentateuch were. Later Emmie was to find an ally, someone who recognized her love of learning and briefly became her mentor, advising her on what to read and lending her books. This was A.L. Smith, whom she met at Somerleyton and on his visits to Teddington. A.L., as he was later known, had fought his way up the school system to academic success and was well aware of the problems faced by young people who had missed out on education. We do not know to what extent she confided in him – probably very little, for the fact is, though she was happy to be encouraged in her leisure reading, she was becoming resigned. She realized it was too late.

Too late for her; but not for Gertrude. Gertrude was her closest sister. They shared a room, and in their correspondence they used spoof endearments for each other such as mediaeval knights might (supposedly) address to their lady-loves, taking names out of Gertrude's plays and romances. Emmie, alone among the sisters, was deeply intimate with Gertrude's thought processes, and when Gertrude ('my Dotina') was singled out to go to school, Emmie seemed in some way to feel that she would be educated for both of them.

Gertrude had a mania for learning, Emmie says in her diary. There is a nice description of her in her bedroom in the holiday house in Wales, 'writing crabbily'. It must have been hard to find uninterrupted moments in that large family. Gertrude increasingly used her imagination as an escape; and with her mother tutting over her studying there must have been times when reading and story-writing had the allure of forbidden territory. Emmie was inclined to agree with her mother: 'Gertrude has not been quite well lately, she will work so hard and pore over her books.' Perhaps because of that she had developed round shoulders, as if – living so vividly in her imagination – she wanted to crouch over her fantasies to shield them from the world.

Unlike her two elder sisters, Gertrude did not keep a diary. All her writing energies went into letters and novels. These stories are incomplete; only portions of them have survived. They are written with very few corrections, in a clear, youthful but stylish handwriting; and though all fictional they form a kind of journal at one remove. Through Gertrude's creations we can try to puzzle out the kind of person she was.

Her total *œuvre* that has come down to us consists of two sketchbooks, a portfolio of about ten pictures: watercolours, depicting dramatic Gothic scenes (these were the pictures that I was allowed to look at after lunch with my grandmother), part of three novels, *The Baroness Eugenie*, *Dorothea* and an untitled novelette about the Jacobite rebellion of 1745, and a play, *The Fanatic*, about the Civil War, which she and Mary wrote together.

Gertrude was 17 when she died. She had been away at school for just under a year during which she had not written anything. So this output (and probably more – there are surely other plays that are lost) represents about four years' work, the fruit of her early teens. *The Fanatic* is probably the earliest of the four. *Baroness Eugenie* was completed in April 1872 (she dated it) when she was 13½, *Dorothea* begun a month later. We have the last volume of *Baroness Eugenie* and the first volume of *Dorothea* ('a Novel in 10 numbers and 2 volumes').

The Baroness Eugenie is a mediæval romance, full of gallant rescues and hair's-breadth escapes. The leading characters include the 'peerless English knight' Sir Hugh, the cunning 'supposed harper' Gilbert ('As agile as a monkey, in a minute he had climbed the wall . . . jumped down into the stable . . . and in a few minutes was riding like the wind, and leaping fearlessly over culls and ditches till at length the earl's castle stood, stately and grim before him') and the eponymous Eugenie, the 'haughty' Baroness who gets her come-uppance with an early end and deathbed repentance (it is a moral tale). What is similar in the two novels, this one and *Dorothea*, is that in each Gertrude knows exactly where she is going. They have a cracking pace, the action develops fast from the first page and their solemn intent seems secondary to the sheer fun of story-telling. But at the end of *Eugenie* we are reminded of its moral sub-agenda: 'Now, Reader, you must bid adieu to these characters, they are but poorly painted but they are the first attempts of an Author, who has tried humbly to bring before the Reader the awful effects of jealousy' (thus the 13-year-old author; who, one wonders, was she jealous of – the pretty little Lilian, four years her junior, or the bossy eldest sister always ready to reprove her?) *Dorothea* begins with a similar caution: 'In writing this book I have not been without a purpose and I earnestly trust, not only a moment's interest but a lesson may be drawn from these pages. It has been my intention to show the effects of an idly spent life, too much novel reading and romantic dreams on a girl's mind.' The next sentence, though, tempers the message: 'Not that I condemn sweet dreams. Many imaginations, castles in the air, are the sweetest part of a young creature's existence. But when carried too far by want of other exercise of the mind, or with thinking too much of self, they become dangerous.'

Gertrude was a devout church-goer. We have her mission card, like Emily's, dedicating her to the Christian life of being good and putting others before herself: 'I, Gertrude Alice Baird . . . do resolve to think less of myself, more of others, and especially to cultivate the spirit of humility, obedience, reverence and love towards my parents.' But like Mary, in the latter's response to the touch of an admirer's hand, Gertrude becomes herself (or another side of herself) at the touch of pen and notebook. Writing is her passion. Reading *Dorothea* you sense it is written for the sheer joy of it and an amazing achievement it, or the half of it that has survived, is for a 13-year-old.

She is totally confident on paper, this shy round-shouldered girl. Of course the style is derivative – she was reading *Middlemarch, The Cloister and the Hearth* and *Mansfield Park –* but the book's tight structure, characterization and the sheer competence of the writing are all her own.

Take its opening: 'It was early in the afternoon, one of those dull London afternoons, when the hot summer sun beats on the pavements, when not a cloud is in the smoky sky, and when dust and heat prevail everywhere.' The scene is set, and we go to Waterloo station where Dolly, our heroine, is about to catch a train to Kent. Quite a number of people who are going to be important to the plot are on that train, a useful device for pulling the story together. Twelve-year-old Dolly is in mourning: 'The neglected untidy way in which she was dressed too plainly showed the absence of a mother's care.' Her only luggage is an overflowing carpet-bag with 'a white nightgown and something red peeping out of it'. That red something catches our eye, so when we are told Dolly is reading a novel (here it comes) called *The Ocean Demon* we have no difficulty imagining its cover. And this same novel is noticed by a young boy in the same compartment. A dialogue ensues between the children, listened to by an elderly lady who is travelling with her lapdog. The boy notices Dolly's luggage label:

'Dorothea Amstead,' said he reading, 'is that your name?'

'Yes, I'm called after my aunt, whom I'm going to visit – to stay with always.'

'Oh!' said he abruptly. 'I don't like that name, it's like Bridget and Phoebe and all the rest of them.'

Miss MacKenzie [the old lady] . . . heard him say this, and he fell in her estimation, for it must be confessed that her own name was Bridget.

'Well,' continued the schoolboy, 'as you've told me your name I'll tell you mine, it's plain Tom Richardson, and I've got a sister Emmeline, perhaps that name pleases you.'

'Yes. But your name is like Willie, Johnnie, Peter and all the rest of them.'

They both laughed.

The gleam of humour throughout this exchange is in sharp contrast to the melodramatic intensity of the Baroness Eugenie. Though the book's opening has resonances of Wilkie Collins (see the beginning of *The Woman in White*) and the description of Dolly's aunt and her family, the Merivales, 'who thought themselves, and were regarded, as the principal people in the neighbourhood', has a Jane Austenian irony, Gertrude's sense of the comic is very much her own, a strand in her personality which her letters don't show, nor the references about her in her sisters' diaries.

Dolly is an heiress; her rich father has left the Merivales £5,000 a year to cover the cost of her upkeep (the equivalent of about £45,000, a measure of how out of touch the Baird girls were with the value of money). The Merivales have six children (like the Bairds), the second of whom, Connie, takes Dolly under her wing. Connie likes arguing: 'It was one of Connie's peculiaritys [sic] that she thought everybody wrong who did not hold the same opinion as herself.' (Is this a portrait of Mary?). Connie takes Dolly to church, 'an old fashioned building. . . . The walls were yellow with age, and covered with tablets representing gouty cherubs holding manuscripts. . . . The windows were all of blue glass, except one which boasted a tiny picture of a small saint with large hands. This was regarded by the old rector as popery, and it was always going to be pulled down, whenever he preached of popery (which was his favourite subject). He hammered at the desk and looked at the offending window, and scowled at the shrinking saint.'

The images – gouty cherubs, the shrinking saint with the large hands, the scowling rector – are vivid. This is a girl who knows how to use language; and the colours in her description (the ageing yellow of the walls, the blue of the glass) are chosen with the eye of a painter. She is equally sure in her vignette of the two girls and their relationship:

Dolly was not clever, yet she could not be called stupid. Day by day her friendship with Connie grew stronger. Connie wrote poems, a thing Dolly could never do, but her admiration of them was without envy. Connie too was romantic but more animated than Dolly; thus the friendship increased between them and the sentimental nonsense they talked could have filled many a volume.

In a religious fit the two girls decide to do good by giving some old stockings to the worthy gardener's daughter ('Mama would like us to be charitable'), only to discover the stockings were not old and were needed at home; the governess, Miss Prim, gives them a good wigging. So, mortification – and the girls have to retrieve the stockings. We are told, 'It was a long time before they tried 'charity' again.

We next see Dolly four years later; she is 'still the same shadowy little creature, with large dark eyes'. At a croquet party – 'of course Mr Graham the curate was there, and the three young Mr Browns, for as there was a lack of gentlemen in the neighbourhood they attended every party' (shades of Teddington?) – Dolly meets a tall handsome youth 'with a Spanish look about him'. Enter Anthony Turner, the villain in hero's clothing. From then on there are three strands to the story: Dolly's infatuation with the said Anthony, the marriage of Dolly's ne'er-do-well brother Granville to a saintly girl called Mabel and the faithful love of Tom Richardson, the boy from the opening scene, now grown up and devoted to Dolly. The story moves swiftly from one subplot to another; every now and then the authorial voice is heard, helping to give us a bird's-eye view of the whole. 'If the reader thinks I say little of the love part of this wedding [of one of the Merivale daughters] it is because of the numerous lovers which follow in after chapters'; and a few pages later, when Granville and Mabel take refuge abroad: 'As all is mystery about them, it is better to unravel my story. I will transport the reader for a few hours to the continent and to the German town of Baden Baden.' Gertrude knows the town well, it has been on many a Baird southward route. The following passage shows her on sure ground:

It was night, the moon shone on the sleeping town of Baden-Baden, it shone down the streets where the gas light still gleamed from the gambling-houses, it shone down the dark and miserable alleys, lighting all with its cold clear light, it shone through the windows in the Baden Hotel where Mabel was sleeping, it lighted up the mother's pale face, as she lay with the infant beside her.

Later, when the luckless couple and child have to do a flit, we get another night-time sketch of the town:

Silently they threaded the streets. Once they passed a house where lights still shone from the windows and the sound of music and merry laughter were heard. . . . They passed a few ginshops where men shouted in drunken mirth. One of these standing outside a shop tried to lift up Mabel's veil and look at her face, and laughed loudly as she rushed away to catch up Granville, pale, shuddering, drawing the baby closely to her. At length they reached the station. It was then nearly two o'clock but still all was noise and confusion there. The train had only just rumbled into the station. After taking their tickets, Granville lifted her in, jumped in himself. And soon the great fiery-eyed train sped onwards through the darkness. Onward! Onward through the starlight night, far away from the town of Baden.

There are plenty of minor characters. We meet the catty Miss Cornelia White (who resembles her sisters, all 'good plain girls in every sense of the word'). Miss Cornelia, as she is known, could be a first cousin of Jane Austen's Lucy Steele. She discovers Dolly's secret (that she, Dolly, is determined to 'refuse' Tom), promises Dolly and Connie she won't tell anyone; but, as she wends her way home, 'the two girls did not see how she giggled to herself, and how her green plumed bonnet bobbed up and down with suppressed laughter'. Again, a splash of colour to catch our attention: the scene is fixed in our mind's eye by that treacherous green plume. Then there is Emmeline, the abandoned wife of the nefarious Anthony, left alone with her ailing child. There is a touching scene when Dolly (unaware of the relationship) comes to her aid and, the child's fever 'crisis' over, Emmeline's emotional relief takes the form of a great surge of love for Dolly: 'What would have been the feelings of the wicked Anthony had he seen his victims sit so lovingly together?'

Dolly's social life takes her on a visit to Lime Hall, the stately home of the Mackenzies (she of the lapdog in the train). Mrs MacKenzie is the author of religious tracts, and thinks rather well of herself as a writer. The company at Dolly's first dinner in the house consists of 'two old ladies and three old gentlemen each one dryer than the other' (reminiscent of that dissenting minister, 'ugly as sin', on one of Mary's Somerleyton trips). The more we hear about Lime Hall the more I picture it as Somerleyton as it was before the addition of a library and the enlightened innovations of its later owners. Dolly feels distinctly cast down. 'There were no books worth mentioning in the house, no pictures but flaring oil paintings from which Dolly, with her true taste for art, shrank. The house was ornamented with every hideos [sic] costly piece of furniture that could be devised, from frightful flaring screens to the rainbow coloured scarlet and magenta carpet.' Dolly spends a dreary Christmas there. 'Mrs Mackenzie argued daily with the third gentleman, and Mr McKenzie tried to enliven them with bad jokes at which nobody laughed but himself.'

Our young author can be quite biting. These observations, like the snide remarks about Miss Cornelia and her sisters' looks, must have been the fruit of many an evening spent silently observing grown-up company. Gertrude drew on her environment for her details, probably without realising where they came from. Anthony, who is shortly going to turn up at Lime Hall, has a charming smile and an invalid father, immediately reminding me (fresh from Mary's diary) of Jerry and his father, but they were probably far away from Gertrude's conscious thoughts as she wrote.

After that dour Christmas, Dolly's mood is transformed by the arrival of the handsome Anthony. They walk in the grounds of Lime Hall, and he gazes into her eyes 'with that fascinating look he could so easily assume', Anthony's strategy is twofold:

to lure Dolly into marriage and to hasten his father's death, which will bring him two windfalls (this is eight years before the Married Woman's Property Act). Anthony woos Dolly with stories of his travels as they walk through the snowy garden: 'He told her of the many Christmas days he had spent in germany [sic], the lovely pine-forests there, and of the lovely swiss [sic] mountains where the snows never melt, and are always pure and white except when tinged with the glow of the setting sun, till Dolly's hazel eyes shone with excitement. . . . Each new word he uttered, like a serpent's coil, wound more closely round the poor child's heart.' His declaration of love leaves Dolly feeling 'she could have died for him'. Shy Dolly is both the fictional girl and Gertrude herself. Dolly – like her creator? – has 'been through the "awkward age" when girls are tortured with dumb-bells and backboards, and when nervous mamas take round-shouldered girls to have their backs examined'. Gertrude knew all about fantasies of romantic love; but she was also writing with an eye on the moral of the story. You feel her heart beating with Dolly's, while her mind warns us of Dolly's blindness. Compassion and detachment – these are the two key ingredients in the book, compassion tempering its morality, detachment its melodrama.

And dramatic, if not melodramatic, it becomes. Anthony has hired a paid assassin to kill his father, a certain Herr Bruger whom we have already met blackmailing Granville in the gambling dens of Baden-Baden. Herr Bruger is 'a short grey-bearded German, [with] small searching eyes peeping from beneath thick iron-grey eyebrows. His features were coarse and bloated. [He] smelt strongly of beer and tobacco.' With Anthony's connivance Bruger gets into his father's house, and the story moves into the dramatic present as Bruger 'glides along the passages of the silent house to the sick man's room. . . . Now

Herr Bruger advances, now he has siezed [sic] the large soft pillow! . . . A stifled groan, a few gasps and the old man is dead! There are no signs of violence on the corpse, the expression of his face, shrunken and yellow, is a strange angry one. Bruger again leaves the house unperceived.'

He leaves the house – and the novel. The notebook, volume one, ends with Granville and Mabel's night departure from Baden. And we are left in suspense, with Anthony still to be unmasked, Herr Bruger with a triumphant sneer on his face, Tom rejected, Granville and Mabel still on the train. Dolly's fate is undetermined, but there is a sentence in the author's foreword which indicates the direction it will take: 'It will be observed that as soon as Dolly beginning a new life works hard as a governess she sees her faults more clearly and does not indulge them again.' She has lost her £5,000 a year, she has become a governess to (perhaps) just such a family as the Baird's, but – surely – the loyal Tom Richardson is still waiting for her. (The romantic bug is catching: I cannot bear the thought that it might not have a happy ending.)

The family were well aware of Gertrude's talent. Her books were read aloud, certainly among the children, as we see from this letter from Gertrude to Emmie written from Somerleyton in July 1972: 'I quite longed to be home when I heard how unwell you were so that I could get out the "little table" and the Baroness Eugenie and hot toast.'). As we have seen, like Emmie she was set on acquiring more learning, that other 'exercise of the mind' that would balance the castles in the air. Her mother might have been in favour in principle but, it seems, was keen to censor the learning process whenever she felt necessary. Gertrude writes a revealing letter to Emmie, again from Somerleyton, in which she begs the latter to intercede for her so that their mother will let her read *Jane Eyre* (why couldn't she ask for herself?): 'I don't see how reading about bad people can make one bad. Baby [Dolly] has not grown wicked because she saw Ralph in the Queen's Revenge [lost play], and as Ralph was only you dressed up, as in books the author often puts in a person in real life with their character faintly disguised', and she draws a picture in the margin of a large book with a diminutive cloaked female figure beside it.

Whatever their mother's scruples, the decision was taken. Uncle William's timely legacy, the prospect of a good school in a healthier part of the country yet not too far away – everything must have seemed to come together that autumn of 1874. The prospectus, when it came, made Albany Villas seem the perfect answer.

Mesdames Collinet (the elder of whom had been the Trollope governess) 'receive a limited number of YOUNG LADIES to instruct in English, French, and the usual branches of Education.' In such a small school Gertrude would not feel lost, there would surely be a family atmosphere. The annual fee of 100 guineas presented no problems. For eight guineas extra each she could also study piano, drawing and painting, German and Italian. Singing would cost a little more, dancing less; there also would be riding (not mentioned in the prospectus) and concerts. She would emerge accomplished, well-educated, confident. Of course the family would miss her, but there were always the holidays.

We do not know which of her parents took her there. No family diaries survive from the period immediately before her departure. They wintered in Teddington that year. William Baird, John Forster's younger brother, the tolerant sermon writer, died of tuberculosis at the end of 1875. We do not know how close the brothers were; there is one account in Emmie's diary of a visit to his parish fete in Homerton at which the girls

(Emmie and Mary) behaved rather badly, giggling at what Mary snobbishly called 'the Homerton elite', while their father behaved with characteristic good manners and amiability. But however much or little an uncle's terminal illness registered with the girls, it could only have struck a note of doom for their father as another member of his family fell victim to the killer disease. 1875 must have been a time of anxiety for him.

I have already suggested that the choice of Albany Villas was probably made on personal recommendation. There were no educational consultants in those days. I have surmised that John Forster Baird heard about it from Anthony Trollope; but if that's so Trollope evidently neglected to tell him that Bice (Beatrice), his niece who had gone there, had hated it (nor probably did Trollope mention that his brother Tom had decided it was immensely expensive, coming to about £275 a year, or that he himself was shocked by how thin Bice had become there). One can imagine the conversation at the Garrick, with Trollope saying he understood the school had improved in recent years – after all, Bice had been there eight years earlier and educational standards could only have gone up, what with the new act and all. Besides, a certain amount of suffering was often regarded as an inevitable and even strengthening part of the boarding school experience. John Forster Baird, remembering his Rugby days, might have reasoned that whatever hardships it might entail they would be nothing to what he had had to go through at a roughly similar age. Besides, a ladies' establishment catering for not more than 20 girls would be a very different thing from a large boys' public school. Most important of all, Gertrude wanted to go. Her 'mania for learning' would be satisfied at last.

So in April 1875 she was installed in 12–13 Albany Villas, Hove. Albany Villas is a broad street of white stuccoed houses running at right angles to the sea. It was much sought after by school-owners. A Miss Wyatt ran another girls' school further up the road and there was also a 'gentlemen's preparatory school'. The crocodile columns of schoolchildren must have come across each other on their way to the sea. Now there are large buildings at the south end of the road blocking off the view of the sea, but in those days it would have been visible from the Collinets' front garden, and the noise of waves and the scream of seagulls part of the background sounds of daily life. The Collinet houses are two large, attached, four-storey houses facing west, with bay windows on the ground floor and handsome stone steps leading up to the two front doors. Gertrude, with all her luggage, would have come by carriage from Hove station, about ten minutes' walk away, or from Brighton. At the bottom of Albany Villas is the King's Road, running along the sea front which connects Hove with the smart part of Brighton, the Regency squares and crescents that were the home of the rich and fashionable, and the shops that catered for them. This might have given the Baird parents pause for thought – would their daughter be tempted to spend too much money? But they knew their Gertrude. She was made in a firmer mould.

Like the other sisters, like anyone, she was many-layered. But whereas with Mary you feel the different facets of her character mesh together – religion, flirtations, teaching, all were a logical outcome of the strong personality and quicksilver intensity of her nature – and with Emmie a docile nature and accepting faith were part of the same weave, with Gertrude you have a sense of contradictions, of hidden qualities which when they surface are at odds with other parts of her. Something bowed her shoulders – just her writing, or was it a sense of her own unworthiness? She had an unusually high forehead framed by long fair to brown, not quite curly hair, the family's generous mouth and wide, slightly deep-set blue eyes. In her photographs she looks beautiful, but she thought she was plain and her mien evidently expressed this. This is how Mary, later, described her: 'Her gentle, wistful ways attracted everyone; [she was] extraordinarily gifted, but at the same time somewhat of a mediaeval mystic in her asceticism.'

Yet this gentle wistful girl had produced that well-written, confident novel and several others too. She could also be a little less than wistful: we have seen what Mary called her 'impertinence' at a moment when I suspect Gertrude simply did not know how to reconcile her own need for time and space with the social demands of family life. The mediaeval mystic side of her may well have served as an unintentional defence: to the Victorians the quiet child was the good child, and good children were left alone. It is this apparent low profile that makes the richness of her writings, not to mention her pictures, all the more remarkable. This, then, was the girl – outwardly shy and undemanding, inwardly burning with a rare creative talent – who found herself at boarding school at the end of April 1875, facing separation from her family for the first time in her life and having to share a room with a complete stranger.

9   *Albany Villas*

'*This hungry place.*'
> Gertrude Baird, in a letter to her sister Emmie,
> October 1875

The stranger was a 17-year-old called Constance Ross. 'Stupid, and dark, but nice,' Gertrude described her. (We do not know what Constance thought of Gertrude.) They both cried under the bedclothes at night but could not talk or even whisper (both were against the rules) so were not able to comfort each other; anyway they were probably too shy and too unhappy to.

'I miss home most in the evenings,' Gertrude wrote in her first letter to Emmie, marking it 'Private'. It was a mixed report she sent. The place was nicer than she'd expected, but she admitted she'd been miserable. She was put in the second class ('learning what I knew already') until an English teacher, the nice Miss Nicholls, came to her rescue and got her moved up. 'The lesson hours are long, but they are not hard, a good deal of it is sitting round a table and answering a question in turn; now and then indeed I have time to draw many pigs in my "cahier de brouillon"' [rough book].

There were 17 boarders at the school in that late spring of 1875, the eldest aged 19, the youngest 12, and three day-boarders aged eight, ten and 12. In her first letter to her mother

Gertrude listed their names and ages, with comments ('nice' or 'pretty'). Some were both nice and pretty, some neither, but 'there is no-one *dislikeable* in the school, and one pretty tall girl I am in love with' (common Victorian parlance for 'I like a lot'). She also reassured Emmie about the food: 'If Mama had seen the dinner today she would not have feared starvation. Roast beef, cold pork, yorkshire pudding, plum pudding, vegetables etc.' The Collinets were evidently putting on a good show for the beginning of term. On the back of the list of pupils Gertrude outlined her daily timetable:

<u>Lesson hours:</u>   7.30 to 8; breakfast at 8
                     8.30 to 12; dinner at 1.30
                     3.30 to 6; tea at 6
                     6.30 to 7; work from 7 till bedtime at 8.

Sundays began with scripture lessons, followed by church; the afternoon was free for walks, then there was church again in the evening, the same kind of routine as at home. But the church and the services were not up to Teddington standards; there were few decorations and the hymns were new to her. Gertrude had evidently struck an unfamiliar strand of Anglicanism on the south coast (or 'the advanced movement' had not yet arrived).

Our sources for these 11 months when Gertrude was at school, from May 1875 to April 1876, are four sets of letters: Gertrude's to her mother, Gertrude's to Emmie, Madame Collinet's to her parents when she first got ill; and finally the grief-stricken letters from her best school friend, Louisa Richardson, to Mary after her death. Each set has its own slant. Gertrude is endlessly reassuring to her parents – only little phrases hint at a darker reality – but her letters to Emmie, as one would expect, give a much fuller picture. While Madame Collinet's ooze unctuous concern, Louisa Richardson's are outpourings of raw grief. What these four collections give us is an intimate view on an almost daily basis of Gertrude's life during her three terms at school: and a fascinating story it is.

Homesickness hit her with the force of a virus, clouding the beginning of each term and even infecting her Northumberland holiday that summer in the anticipation of the next exile. ('I should have liked to run straight back to Bamburgh,' she wrote to Emmie after her return to Albany Villas, 'this is very prisony after the delightful liberty of Bamburgh.') Bamburgh meant running on the beach, hair flying; school was walking in crocodile and rules you broke without realizing. The contrast between home life and the iron rigidity of the Collinet regime would be a shock to any system; but for Gertrude it was profoundly debilitating. She was very much lacking in social confidence. Her inner defence was her creative imagination, but this the school timetable left no time for. The other side of her was the obedient girl, anxious to be liked and do what was expected of her, always ready to think herself in the wrong. In the home setting she might feel safe enough to give vent to 'impertinence' as she had that time in Glion when Mary had had to tick her off, but school was not a safe environment. She was not like one of the other Albany Villas pupils, a certain Ada, who rounded on Madame Collinet saying she hated her and the school (and was duly expelled). Gertrude dealt with her homesickness by assuming that it was her fault, a sign of weakness of character and of her own inadequacy. Nowadays telephone calls and visits would keep the links with home open and active. Gertrude had only letters (rationed to one afternoon a week for writing) and parcels. Furthermore, Madame Collinet slept in the room under Gertrude's and Constance's and had unusually sharp hearing, another factor operating against the exchange of late-night girlish confidences that might have helped her in her first term.

There were three Collinets at Albany Villas: Madame
Collinet, the one-time governess, now school owner and
headmistress, and her two daughters, Mademoiselle Marie and
Mademoiselle Claire. Madame Collinet was probably in her
mid- or late 50s, her daughters in their 30s. Mademoiselle Marie
is the one Gertrude mentions most often; she was the most
sympathetic of the three. Madame Collinet was regarded by the
girls as a dragon, and she ran her establishment with the
arbitrariness of an autocrat. The girls were under a lot of pressure
to work hard. Some of them would get up at 5 a.m. to finish
off their homework, but this was denied to Gertrude because of
the alert Madame Collinet a floor below ('Who was wearing
ploughman's boots?' she would complain if she heard an early-
morning creak of the floorboards). But – this was part of the
arbitrariness too – there could be unexpected holidays, as when
the larger of Madame's two nasty little dogs, which had been
lost, was found. (Later this same dog ate half of Louisa
Richardson's final history essay; the dog was forgiven but Louisa
had to write her essay again.) There were good and bad marks
dealt out daily for behaviour, in addition to the ordinary school
marks: the winner of the most good marks each week was given
a cross and rewarded by supper with Madame in her rooms.
Many of the girls, Gertrude told Emmie, cultivated bad marks
in order to avoid this unwelcome treat: 'We none of us like
kissing her when we say goodnight.' Madame made a subtly
mean swipe at Gertrude on the latter's birthday that autumn:
'Now you have such nice things you must never think of
stooping,' Gertrude reported her as saying. One wonders
whether Emily Baird had written to her about Gertrude's
deportment problem. It is clear that Gertrude realized hers were
not the only letters going between Hove and Teddington: 'Last
night when I kissed Madame she said I must try to be coquet

[feminine]. Did she say I was unpraticle [sic] in her letter? Mlle Marie has got that idea when as monitress I let the fire out and forgot to put the bibles for prayers on the table, so she reproved me. I thought Mother might have suggested it.'

While to her mother Gertrude barely mentioned the school's spartan regime beyond wishing, during a cold spell in October, that the fires could be lit ('this is such cold catching weather'), to Emmie she was more explicit. 'It is rather hard getting up in the mornings now [October 31st]; the great bell in the conservatory rings at six, and the light comes dimly through the shutters, and it is *very* cold,' and later: 'We are not allowed to gather round the fire at lessons but may warm ourselves for 5 minutes and then retire.'

After that initial splendid meal the food became less satisfying, not quite as bad as the burnt porridge in *Jane Eyre*, but certainly less appetizing than home fare. Gertrude was changing physically, growing a fuller figure (she had to let her dresses out). In one of her letters home there is a suggestion, in a comment she makes about her younger sister Lilian, that the latter has started to menstruate while she herself has not. If so, it is possible that the physical changes in her and the resulting appetite were the prelude to menstruation. The weight gain could also have been due to lack of exercise; she was walking much less than at home. The family regularly sent her boxes with clothes (dresses, warm shawls, socks knitted by Mary, dressing-up clothes for school parties) and food, but she cautioned against the latter – the jam, for instance, would disappear and be used instead of school jam. The Collinets ran a tight ship. To Gertrude it was simply 'this hungry place'.

But, once she had settled in, there was an aspect of school that she loved: the lessons. The composition master, who also taught arithmetic and history, was nice, she reported in an early letter home, except that she had been mortified in her first lesson when he had drawn the class's attention to the pig she was doodling in her exercise book (why always pigs?) and everyone had laughed. French and English were '*very* good'; music, though, not nearly as nice as Mr Hopper's lessons at home. (Gertrude had a problem with music: she was supposed to be unmusical and several times she mentions that it is 'wasted' on her, but quite clearly she got enormous pleasure out of the concerts she went to; another example of parental labelling, one feels.) One part of English that initially she found difficult was composition. 'It is dreadful hearing one's compositions criticised,' and worse still was having to read them aloud herself. It seems that no one in the school had been told that she had already written three novels, and she was not going to talk about it. She was just another pupil with sometimes rather dodgy spelling who had to be taught, like them all, to write formal letters and how to structure an essay. (One of her English teachers, Mr Philip, spotted her talent, calling her 'the poetess'. 'Where is our poetess?' he asked in the summer term after her death.)

By the autumn Gertrude was in the first French class; 'a run to the Stag rocks [at Bamburgh] would be a nice change', she added drily, after telling her parents this in her weekly letter home. Looking at her *cahier* one can only agree at the sight of those endless *dictées* and grammatical *analyses*, all beautifully written in her copperplate handwriting. Leafing through those exercise books you can see she is getting a thorough grounding in education: history, English, French and German. Her history book is a gradgrindian list of facts covering huge swathes of English history, her English a dissection of grammar ('subject', 'predicate', 'object') unknown today. But there was no science and no 20th-century history to clutter the Albany Villas' syllabus. English grammar was to Gertrude was what parsing

Latin and Greek had been to her father at Rugby 30 years earlier.

What worried her, however, was that she had no idea where all this education was leading. A few of the girls were going to take the Cambridge examination which, as we have seen, was attracting more entrants every year, some of whom were even going on to university (Girton College had recently been founded). On an afternoon outing to Brighton towards the end of the summer term, Gertrude asked Miss Nicholls if she could take the university exam. An old girl of the school, a certain Florence, had come back to collect the prizes she had won, including her pass in the Cambridge Senior examination. 'She is only 16 and not at all stunted with learning,' Gertrude commented pointedly to her mother in her description of the prize-giving scene. The whole school had trooped 'in procession' to the Pavilion, and the prizes had been given away by the mayor of Brighton. 'So many stupid speeches, returning thanks and seconding them were made that I had time to learn his face.' As was her wont (she put drawings in almost all her letters), she did a sketch of the mayor, rotund and solemn in his mayoral chain.

Miss Nicholls evidently had a soft spot for Gertrude. It was almost certainly her encouragement that gave Gertrude the push she needed to write home about the university exam. But she did not write to her parents, or mention it apart from that oblique remark after the prize-giving. Her approach was through Emmie – Emmie the interceder – her usual tactic when really important matters were at stake. Here is that letter in full. It is typical of the way she wrote, wrapping an urgent message in lots of little detail, as if she dare not expose her hopes to the light of day, or parental rebuff.

June 4 1875. On Saturday afternoon I went shopping with Miss Nicholls, Augusta and Ada. In a fancy workshop I saw a new kind of damask work, flowers and leaves worked in coloured wool and silk on a drab ground, very pretty. [She includes a sketch, adding 'you see, I thought it would do to work for someone'.] Walking with Miss Nicholls we talked about the examinations (remember, this is private) – Miss Nicholls is freckled, with blue eyes, a small nose, she generally smiles, her hair is done in a padded manner, and her voice is loud and somewhat harsh – withal that her knowledge in some branches of learning is very great. I told her how it had long been my desire to go up for a university examination, there is an Oxford [Cambridge?] one next spring that just suits. If only Mama would allow it, I would prepare for it next winter. Don't say anything about it till the holidays, then I shall implore her. It will not be [sic] working harder than I am now, and school agrees with me so well, that I never have aches or pains of any sort – It would be working with an aim too; and Rose [Templar] would go at the same time for the junior examination. Oh! do help me to persuade Mama in the holidays.

School had awoken her ambition. The exam would make sense of the whole thing. It would make sense of her life.

But then we hear no more mention of it till the following year. On January 30th Gertrude wrote to Emmie: 'It is a pity about the examination.' That is all. Mrs Baird had put her foot down. Gertrude also refers to being 'in the dumps' during the summer holidays. One can imagine the scene in Wynding House. Emmie, primed, would approach her mother, and those blue eyes above the aquiline Brinton nose would widen in amazement and consternation, perhaps even derision. 'Gertrude? taking the university examination! Listen Emmie – isn't that child round-shouldered enough? No, I will not have her doing more work! That school. . . !' One can hear the note of reproach, and perhaps the appeal to her husband ('John, listen to this. . . .'); and while John would give a deprecating shrug, Emmie would climb those shallow stairs to inform her sister. No university examination. So that was Gertrude's 'dumps' in the summer before she died.

(History almost repeated itself 37 years later when my mother, determined to take the Cambridge examination, had ferocious arguments with her mother, Mary, who said she could not go to college unless she won a scholarship, perhaps assuming she would not get one. But my mother did; so that part of the Emily Baird legacy was finally laid to rest.)

There is one telling sentence in Louisa Richardson's letters to Mary after Gertrude's death in which Louisa says, 'On Sundays she used to draw such dear little boys on top of her letters to her mother because she said Mrs Baird was *so* fond of little boys.' Had Emily Baird thought, long ago in 1858, after two daughters, 'this time it must be a boy,' and did disappointment at Gertrude's gender perhaps lead to extra-harsh treatment in childhood, making this most talented of all her daughters develop the low self-esteem shown in her unconfident posture? Gertrude had a deep desire to please her mother and lacked Mary's openly fighting spirit. Whereas Mary could always bounce back after confrontation with her mother and bouts of 'soul-brushing' (a favourite phrase of hers), Gertrude accepted all reproofs as merited. A turning-point for her had been her confirmation, she told Louisa. But if it helped her to feel closer to the comforts of Christianity, it also made her more self-critical, and this she did not need.

After her mother had decided the Cambridge exam was not for her, it seems she lost her sense of direction. 'Work is not so much for a purpose now,' she wrote to Emmie, adding 'I shall wait now till I am 25.' It is not clear why she specified the age of 25; perhaps she was thinking that if she had not married by then her mother would have consigned her to old-maid status, and she might be free to do as she liked. Perhaps she also knew there was some money in the pipeline for the girls. (In fact John Forster Baird, who had evidently succeeded in breaking the male entail set up in the first Baird will, left £150 a year to his daughters on marriage or when they reached the age of 20, not 25.)

Angry though we may feel on Gertrude's behalf, Emily Baird's attitude would have been shared by most Victorian mothers, for whom the word 'bluestocking' struck a note of doom. The chances of marriage would be seriously diminished for a daughter who had turned into one; no middle-class male in his senses wanted a seriously educated wife. A generation earlier Fanny Trollope, Anthony's mother, had noted that for English girls (unlike their French counterparts) 'the terror of being called learned is in general much more powerful than that of being classed as ignorant'. Late Victorian Britain might have been full of powerful female role models trumpeting the need for girls' education, but Emily Baird came from a quiet cultural backwater where people knew their place – men, women, servants – and stayed there. Mary, 50 years and one world war later, answering someone who remarked on the fact that all but one of her seven daughters had married Balliol men, quipped: 'I husband my resources!' It could have been her own mother talking. But what Mary said with humour, her mother believed in deadly earnestness. In the end it was an economic matter. A middle-class woman without an adequate private income married, became a governess or starved. The Forster-Baird clan had produced several unmarried women, supported by their fortunately well-off relations. Mrs Baird's job as a Victorian mother was indeed to husband her resources, which meant turning her daughters into marriageable commodities. Gertrude was an odd enough girl already.

There might have been another worry on Emily's mind. While she was fighting her rearguard action against the forces of liberal education, her brother John Brinton was engaged in the industrial dispute that had hit the headlines of *Le Figaro*. The mid-1870s saw the beginning of what was called the great depression when, after decades of expansion, prices and profits began to fall. The causes were complex – tariff barriers abroad, increased competition resulting from new technology at home – but the net result was that a manufacturer like John Brinton saw the profits from his looms dwindle frighteningly; and he came up with the clever ruse of sacking his male workers and employing women instead so that labour costs would be cut. News of these troubled times and the crisis at the Brinton factory surely reached the Bairds. It would have reinforced Emmie's decision not to launch her sensitive third daughter into an uncertain future career.

Gertrude took her mother's decision stoically. But it made the return to Albany Villas that September (leaving the rest of the family in Bamburgh; she was taken south by Auntie Jane) almost as bad as the first term. 'It is very dreadful at first, being here after those nice long holidays,' she wrote in her first letter home. The work was harder, but the pressure to do well no longer had the same urgency. In her second letter home, on September 25th, she talked about when she should leave school: 'Please Mama do tell me truthfully whether you would like me to come home for good at Christmas or finish the year here.' But it seemed her parents too were in limbo. Nobody had decided how long her schooling should last; and she was to ask the same question at the beginning of the following term: 'Do tell me if I really leave school at Easter; I thought it was fixed, but . . . Mlle Marie said it was not quite settled as you might not travel. . . . I hope it is a mistake, *do let* me come home for good at Easter.' The final decision, that she should indeed leave that Easter, seems to have been dictated by the family plans for the early summer (they were going to Schwalbach, a spa town where Emily's neuralgia could be treated). Gertrude's education could be wound up so long as it fitted in with the family travel plans.

The focus of her school life now became social rather than

academic. In the autumn term she shared her dormitory with three other girls: Constance, Louisa Richardson and a certain Katie, all nice girls, Gertrude told Emmie – there was a screen for them to dress behind, she said; besides, it was generally dark when they got up. Louisa, who at first she thought talked too much, was now proving her worth; she made them laugh, which helped with bedtime blues. ('There is something so nice and straightforward about her, her spirits are almost too good and the way she laughs is quite infectious.') By the end of term Louisa, who must have had a motherly streak and as we shall see came to adore Gertrude, was tucking her up at night. Gertrude had at last found a friend.

It was not easy for her, particularly as she knew (she admitted this in a letter to Emmie) this had been part of her mother's scheme for her: 'Mama wrote to me to "make friends all round". I am afraid she thinks being at school changes people, but though I get on with the others very well, I have not the slightest idea how to make friends with them. I hope Mama will not be angry with me.' That was in May. By the following autumn she was more open to friendship – and perhaps, with the collapse of her hopes, needed it more.

In spite of the daily eight hours' study there were plenty of opportunities for the girls to get to know each other outside the classroom. When the weather was good they went on weekend walks and expeditions into the countryside; there were strolls down to the beach and swimming (from a bathing machine); there were the regular 'poor-work' evenings when the girls would sew in the big front room with the double doors and chat or read aloud; and there were parties and charades, dances and concerts to celebrate the end of term or the frequent birthdays (which made heavy demands on her purse – several times she had to write home for more pocket money). Recreation, if not always fun, was a regular feature of life at Albany Villas. Gertrude sent home some vivid descriptions home of these organized events.

The first country expedition had been by train from Cliftonville to Bramber with its 'fields full of buttercups and cows grazing in them and hawthorn hedges and shady lanes'. The girls ate their sandwiches under the ruin of Bramber castle, 'then Mlle Marie gave us permission to run wild all over'. They picked armfuls of bluebells, made friends with a village child whom they fed with buns and explored an isolated church where Mabel Archer played the harmonium. Gertrude added sketches: the castle, the child sitting with its legs stuck out in front of it and its mouth full of bun. (Letter-writing time was never long enough, but she always managed to fit in these quick illustrations.) On the next picnic, a month later, they travelled in two waggonets across the downs to Parham Park which they visited, admiring the pictures. This time the green lanes were full of wild roses. Again they gathered flowers (no wonder there are so few today) and as the sun set behind the rolling Sussex hills Gertrude told the other girls their fortunes, 'making up all kinds of things about the lines in their hands and they believed that it was all real fortune telling'.

She was becoming more at ease with her peers. But in spite of these (rare) expeditions further afield, Hove still felt like a prison: 'There is a sameness in our walks, down the road by the sea, meeting heaps of bath chairs and schools, past the pier and home by the other side of the road; one day into the country between flat barren fields, the next we are allowed "out of rank" and gather daisies by the roadside, far off we can see a line of hills, and I suppose that behind them lie woods, but trees are scarce on this side.' On one poor-work evening in December she wrote a typical Baird scene-set: 'This is poor night, the lamps are lighted on the long schoolroom tables, and almost everyone is either sewing or knitting. Miss Nicholls is sitting on one side of me cutting out frocks, Mlle Marie is reading aloud, on the other side of me sits Mabel [Archer] finishing her French composition. . . . She has tied a handkerchief round her head to keep the noise from disturbing her.' Gertrude draws a quick sketch of Miss Nicholls and of Mabel with the handkerchief over her ears.

That autumn, with her hopes about the exam dashed, she spent night hours awake, imagining the distant sound of the sea was Bamburgh. She described one equinoctial storm in a letter to Emmie: 'I heard the sea roaring in the night, and the moonlight through the shutters made ladders of light on the ceiling, and Katie talked in her sleep.' Simple, poetic language; the writer in her is still very much alive.

Louisa Richardson's spontaneous affection was helping her during that depressing term. Louisa gives a vivid and moving account of their friendship in the letters she afterwards wrote to Mary; but Gertrude hardly mentions their friendship in any of her letters home. According to Louisa it was intense. The two girls loved each other as only two teenagers can, as Mary Ann Evans (George Eliot) had loved her friend Sara Hennell, telling her: 'I sometimes talk to you in my soul as lovingly as Solomon's Song.' Such hyberbole was the accepted language of young women's friendships at that time. We meet it in Louisa's letters – a deep love, made even more intense by her despairing sense of bereavement. Gertrude, though, in her letters home, even her private ones to Emmie, presents Louisa as just another friend, the one of the three in her room whose laughter helps keep her happy. This points to a certain imbalance in the relationship, that Louisa loved Gertrude 'more' than Gertrude loved her, but it was also a reflection of their different temperaments. 'No two natures could outwardly be more different than Gertrude's and Louisa's,' wrote Mme Collinet to Mrs Baird. Louisa was the total extrovert. Her feelings tumbled out of her (her grief pours in torrents on to the pages of her letters to Mary, the 'dear Miss Baird' to whom alone she can confide her sense of irreparable loss). Gertrude, on the other hand, whose shyness made the other girls see her as melancholy and sad, trusted her own feelings less, or was less ready to express them. After all, she had her family to fall back on and a loving sister (Emmie) to supply the role of confidant, both elements Louisa lacked. The latter had a sister, 'the queer Anna who left' (Gertrude's words) but the two were not close. Much of Louisa's life had in fact been spent as visiting niece at St Augustine's, Canterbury, where her uncle, Henry Bailey, was warden of the missionary college. But if Louisa's extroversion was a cover for loneliness and Gertrude's reserve rooted in strong family bonds, there was nonetheless a point where each girl needed exactly what the other offered in that alien environment, an intimate and trusting love.

Today their friendship, with its strongly physical expression, might be given a more defining name. Its style, however, was perfectly in tune with the fashion of the time. Physical demonstrativeness between young women – hand-holding, hair-stroking – was regarded as quite natural. Louisa's description of her and Gertrude's closeness is reminiscent of Jane Eyre and Helen Burns at Lowood, where Jane would lie in Helen's lap while the latter stroked her hair. Each pair of girls, one real, the other fictional, was incarcerated in an all-female setting. Each was emerging out of adolescence into womanhood. Nothing was more natural than that they should fall in love. How Gertrude's relationship with Louisa would have developed, we can only imagine. At that stage Gertrude was frightened at the idea of marriage or 'knowing a man' as she put it to Louisa. Whether later life would have reinforced that fear, or she would have gone the Mary way, we will never know.

From Louisa's letters we see the extent to which Gertrude's shyness was a trial to her. 'She tried so hard to conquer being so,' Louisa wrote. Louisa did her best to help by telling her she loved her as she was: 'Sometimes in the school-room, when quite alone with me she would put her head up and walk across the room and ask me if that was how she should do it, and she looked so lovely then.' But it seems Gertrude could only hold her head up high in the safety of Louisa's company; her friend's encouragement had to compete with Madame's digs and a lifetime's labelling. We also hear from Louisa about Gertrude's humility: the little angel-in-the-house acts which showed she was never happy putting herself forward, even to the point where she hoped others would get higher marks than her.

This is Louisa's story: Gertrude seen through the eyes of a girl brought up (partly) by a missionary uncle. Louisa's letters are laced with references to religion, prayers and acts of self-denial, while Gertrude's, interestingly, hardly refer to religion. Neither girl makes any mention of Gertrude's writing; that was not part of Louisa's image of her, and maybe not even part of Gertrude's own reduced self-image then.

On one of the last days before Gertrude fell ill Louisa surprised her alone in their room: 'As I went into the bedroom I saw Gertrude before the window, looking out, her lips were moving and I'm sure she was praying. She started as I came in and as she was just going out & standing for a second by the door she put her arms round me & led me [to] a chair where she sat down & I was kneeling by her & her head was leaning on me, she said as if saying "I am sorry to leave you" "Oh, Louie, *vous êtes très gentille*," those were her words. I'll never forget them.'

Such free expression of affection was something new to Gertrude. She rarely kissed her sisters, she told Louisa; kissing was not customary among the Bairds. (Perhaps their puritanical mother considered such gestures of affection improper.) Louisa's more demonstrative style of friendship was, interestingly, not discouraged by the school. 'In the evening Gertrude would sit on a low cane chair while I sat on an ordinary high one, and then she would lean her head against me and I would have my arm around her,' and when they said goodnight, 'she [Gertrude] would open her arms so wide and clasp me *so* close and thus we would stay for some time . . . then I would kiss her dear hands all over and she did mine once or twice, but I liked kissing her best, for I was not worthy of her kisses.' (Of Gertrude's hands, Louisa says: 'I loved them the first moment I saw them, there was something in them, so calm, so holy. They were such a lovely brown and so well formed.') One Sunday evening, she told Mary, they had the following conversation: 'As we were sitting together, I with my arm around Gertrude and she leaning her head against me I said, "I should like to be a man, then I should marry you." "Would you, with *all* my faults, knowing them as you do?" I said. Oh! What could I say but "Yes" and then I asked her if *she* would marry me and she answered "Yes".'

Louisa, afterwards, felt she had loved Gertrude 'too much, too wild'. It was possibly a sense of this wildness that made Gertrude hold back from telling her family about their friendship. Total acceptance by one of one's peers can only be a source of support; lover-like adulation such as Louisa's can be a pressure. Did the intensity of Louisa's love bruise, ever so slightly, that deep reserved soul of hers?

Gertrude was grappling with many different stresses during those last months at school. Hard work, sadness about the university exam, uncertainty about when she was going to leave, the pulse-quickening confusion of a passionate friendship – no wonder she could barely hint at any of it, even to Emmie, in her letters home.

By the beginning of March 1876 the end of term was in view. 'I am very glad that half term [sic] is in sight,' she wrote to her mother, 'and that I am coming home for good', though this, in fact, had not been decided yet; she added, 'if Emmie longs for home after her short visit [to Brinton relations], what must I feel'. There were the end-of-term exams to be got over; meanwhile she was not allowed to go to church because of a slight cough ('I feel very heathenish, this is the third Sunday away from church'), but she was allowed to do lessons. The Collinets gave her breakfast in bed; perhaps the cough was worse than Gertrude let on. On March 12th she was writing that she was up and '*perfectly* well. . . . The whooping cough is quite gone; indeed there is not the slightest reason to be fussed about me, my eyes are quite recovered too.'

So, the cat was out of the bag. Madame Collinet wrote apologetically explaining that one other pupil had had the illness and it had been difficult to diagnose; by the time the coughs had turned to whoops the harm had been done. But 'dear Gertrude' was now in the clear, the Bairds had no need to worry, the doctor had been called in and was satisfied the complaint was taking its most favourable course. Gertrude 'looks more ailing and languid than she really is,' a remark of such arrogance and stupidity one marvels that the Bairds did not get on the first train and bring her home at once.

But the Bairds had their own problems. The two younger children were getting ill and soon they would be starting to whoop. It was an epidemic; and a two-year-old with whooping-cough was no joke. Furthermore Emily was in the early months of pregnancy again, often not the best time even for a seasoned child-bearer like her. There were strong reasons for Gertrude's parents to let the anodyne letters from Madame Collinet allay their anxieties. And the bland reports continued. Four days later came another one: '[Gertrude] seems to be progressing fast towards recovery but is worrying herself with the idea that you are anxious . . . and think her more seriously ill than she really is.'

It was quite clear, though, that Gertrude was actually worse; but Madame C. had an answer for that: 'It was to be expected that the complaint would run its usual course and that Gertrude would be worse before she got better. . . . Since I wrote on Sunday she has been so poorly we insisted on her remaining in bed.' She had had a high fever, 'but today Dr Dill found her much better. . . . I hope to be able, in a few days, to write that Gertrude is quite recovered.'

Two days later she was up and dressed but still confined to her room. 'It is better to be a little over-careful than take any risks,' Madame Collinet purred. 'Gertrude is such a favourite that everyone will be glad to see her about the house again. A better, more conscientious girl it would be difficult to find.' This letter coincided with one from Gertrude: 'All that remains of my cough is a cold in the head, I am up, only breakfast in bed and that is ridiculous. It was only a slight form of whooping cough, if that at all, for it is gone.'

Nonetheless, a week later she was still in her room. There had been a change in the weather, it was snowing, Mlle Marie had said she should have an egg for tea ('but I would much rather have bread, like the others. . . . A cake would be nice,' she had written earlier, 'but it might be taken for lunch'). By March 27th the Bairds had decided to act. Emily wrote to Madame Collinet, and later the same day telegraphed, to say that they were coming to Brighton. Mme C. responded with lightning speed: 'I hope this may reach you in time to prevent your coming.' There was no necessity for the journey, Gertrude was progressing steadily; if she stayed in bed for breakfast, that was only to ensure the house had a chance to warm up before she came down, the doctor was satisfied there was 'no disease in the respiratory system'. She was sorry, Mme C. added, 'that you have had coughs at home'.

The Baird visit did not materialize. In her last letter before the end of term Madame Collinet warned that though Gertrude still looked pale and languid it could be due to the exams; her appetite had returned and in fact 'she seems to have nearly regained her usual state of health. . . . You may have heard,' she added in an afterthought, 'that we have a pupil laid up with measles. . . . As we keep the one patient quite isolated, we hope the infection may not spread.' She had not told them before so as not to worry them.

On April 12th Gertrude left Hove for good after a final concert the night before when she played a duet on the piano with another girl. It had gone quite well, in spite of her 'spiritless' playing in the practice. She wrote farewell letters to the Collinets in French: '*Je vous remercie beaucoup pour toute votre bonté*' ('I thank you very much for all your kindness'). Her family were going to travel in May, she said: '*Le changement d'air fera du bien à mes petites sœurs, qui souffrent terriblement de la coqueluche*' ('The change of air will be good for my little sisters who have very bad whooping cough'). '*Coqueluche*' was a word she knew well by then.

She was met at Clapham Junction, off the 12.01 from Brighton, and brought back to Teddington. We have to go back to Mary's journal (already quoted) to remind ourselves how she appeared to her family: 'Ap.12. Gertrude came home today for good, looking very ill, so blue and thin.' Then, five days later,

'Gertrude awoke very spotty'; and another five days later: 'Mr Hoberton was very grave over her *dreadful* throat today. . . . He says if it is not diphtheria it is a close imitation of it.'

She was back in the bosom of her family. And, in the bosom of her family, where two children were recovering from whooping-cough, another was about to go down with measles and one other as well as her had diphtheria, on that bright spring morning of April 29th, she died.

The experiment with education was over.

10 *Mourning*

A year of anxiety and sorrow.
Mary Baird, diary entry, December 3rd 1876

The letters of condolence poured in. The Collinets wrote, as did Gertrude's schoolfriends and the housekeeper from Albany Villas, while Louisa poured out about 12,000 words to Mary in 14 letters over two months. Emily Baird bound her set (including Louisa's to Mary). Emmie did likewise with her collection of Gertrude's letters from school. These are the collections which give us our detailed knowledge of Gertrude's last 18 months, and from them we see the devastation caused by her death.

It was not like our sceptical world today. They all knew, without a shadow of doubt, that she had gone to a better place. As Marie Collinet put it, '[We are] grieved to the heart. Not for the dear one who is gone, for she is beyond doubt happier now than she ever would have been in this world for which she never appeared to be fitted', a thought echoed by Mabel Archer: 'She is far happier now in this world for which she was never fit.' (They must have discussed this in school; it's unimaginable today that one would ever write this to a bereaved parent.) Miss Nichols did not agree. Her letter, from the heart, spoke of a 'beloved pupil', full of promise: 'Never have I had a pupil so good, amiable and conscientious. . . . I loved her dearly.'

Receiving the letters, answering them, sending photographs to Gertrude's school friends, all this occupied the family during the sad days after the funeral. Mary in particular had a heavy task (or was it therapeutic?) answering Louisa's. Louisa admitted that if she had not had the solace of these letters she would have gone out of her mind: 'I long to die and join her,' she wrote. Her aunt and uncle in Canterbury were very kind, they excused her from her social duties, but no one understood what she was feeling; Mary alone was let into her mourning soul.

On top of the sheer shock there was a sense of guilt. 'I know I ought to be thankful for her,' Louisa wrote, 'but it is *so* hard at first, do pray for me that I may be able to say "Thy will be done". . . . We cannot indeed wish her back again.' But they did, of course; how could they not? And back at school again in May, Louisa relived her initial bereavement. 'Sometimes I feel as if I *must* see her come into the room, in her quiet gentle way, and when by her bed the other night I could not believe that her dear arms would never open to take me close to her and that I should never be able to kiss her again. . . . Every minute makes me feel what a blank life is without her.'

Her words burn the page. We must imagine Mary, in the quiet of her room at night or some corner of the garden, reading them, page after page, from the first formal 'Dear Miss Baird' to the later 'Dear Mary' whose sympathetic replies have unleashed this stream. Louisa was going to come and stay, she longed to meet the rest of the family ('I feel I know you all so well'), then it had to be put off. She finally came in August. Mary went to Clapham Junction to meet her and seems to have monopolized her, to the exclusion of Emmie, until Louisa was moved in with the latter, having been heard crying in her room which was the one where Gertrude had died. (Louisa, according to Emmie's diary, 'had a feeling it had happened there. . . . It felt so lonely without Gertrude, she missed her so, Mary could not bear to leave her to cry by herself.')

Louisa, or Louie as the girls called her, was very unBaird-like in both temperament and physique. She was 'rather plump, with lovely soft brown hair and brown eyes . . . and a sweet expression in them,' Emmie reported; and she was a great weeper. Not only in her room and alone with Mary or Emmie, but at church too on Sunday morning. Emmie 'felt *so sorry* for her' during this outburst but noted that it had made Louisa feet better – as in fact they all did. They showed her Gertrude's sketchbooks and writings, they spent hours beside her grave, they went to a moving evening service in the new church, St Peter and Paul, and sang hymns as it got dark ('no gas was lit'), one of which, 'O God, this night', Gertrude had often sung to herself as she got ready for bed. All this, Emily reported, left her feeling 'quite happy and at peace' for the first time for months.

We hear no more about Louisa until she becomes one of the godparents to the last Baird baby, born a few weeks after her visit. She is a poignant figure, this pretty, loving, emotional girl. She flits into our story briefly then disappears; and, strangely, as at the beginning when she isn't mentioned in Gertrude's letters home, she makes no appearance in Mary's diary. Mary got a letter every other day from her (and what letters – the first one is 13 pages long), but there is no mention of them in her diary. This was a moment of huge crisis for Louisa, which touched, directly, the crisis in the Bairds' life. But she was not central to their lives as they, momentarily, were to hers. Like all large families they were wrapped up in themselves, and never more so than when tragedy struck.

They had all gone into mourning, which they had only just stepped out of that Easter after Uncle William's death; even little two-year-old Dolly wore a black sash on her white pinafore. Mourning, in fact, was a regular part of their lives. They were wearing black in Switzerland in 1872 (for Uncle Frank Crossley), then again on their way to Bamburgh a year later (for Aunt Anna-Maria Baird). Official mourning was big business in the 19th century, helped by the example of a queen who had prolonged her mourning after being widowed in 1861. The complete rig was awesome: dress of black paramatta (light wool and silk) with skirt and bodice covered with crepe. Full mourning would be worn for a year by a widow, six months by children, followed by half mourning (lighter colours) for the second year or second six months. By coincidence John Forster Baird's proof copy of his Tyrolean guidebook contains an advertisement for 'domestic mourning' (i.e. for servants) at Jay's in Regent Street: 'Under servants, silk and crape bonnets, 15s 6d. Upper servants ditto, 18s 6d.'

The Bairds, though, were having none of that. At Gertrude's funeral there were no black hat-bands and everybody carried white flowers. The dark dress which Mary donned as soon as she was up from the measles was just that, a simple black dress. But though she might not have put on full mourning, and her grief was less open and vociferous than Louisa's, she was nonetheless flattened by it. As were they all.

Here is Mary, on her first visit to the church after her illness: 'I stayed long at Gertrude's dear grave. . . . Is it really our Doty, one of us, who is lying there? I must write this question: it keeps coming again and again into my head', and a month later: 'It is a *very* weary world, alas! I feel as if I had lived my life, all the pleasant part of it; nothing is before me but blank years of sorrow.' A few weeks later Emmie writes: 'It is not quite two months since dear Doty's death, it feels much longer – and I feel years older. I think I have realized her death, though, now –

sometimes it comes over me with an inexpressibly dreary feeling that I can never have her again here, never hear her talk, or feel her dear hand gently placed in mine; or stroking my hair, as last year when I was miserable. I could not talk to anyone as I could to her, I was sure of sympathy and advice from her – I feel as if I were drifting about, having lost my anchor. . . . Mary is very very sweet and nice, but she can never be to me what Gertrude was.'

It had aged them all – their father visibly: he had newly greying hair. Their mother seems to have been in some ways the best protected, insulated both by pregnancy and her unshakeable faith (remember her first words to Mary, that it was sacrilege to disturb the sleep of such happy dead). But for the two elder sisters it was a watershed in their growing up. Emmie matured, overnight, into greater resignation and a conscious desire to model herself on her dead sister by being a better and more caring person. She increasingly developed a serene and quiet confidence (qualities that in later years made her a favourite aunt to her nieces.)

Mary was deeply unhappy, with herself and with the people around her. Her diary reveals that she still had religious doubts – not about her basic faith but about her ability to translate that into acceptable everyday behaviour. She crossed swords with her mother on an almost daily basis, two impatient women snapping like turtles at the slightest provocation. Her frustration at her mother's abrasive manner is easy to understand, though one has to remember that Emily was pregnant in an exceptionally hot summer, and however light her black dresses and petticoats they were not that light. But one other thing Mary's diary shows, underneath all the soul-talk and questionings: a sense of time. The death of a sister had an urgent message for her. Her next birthday would be her 21st, a landmark for anyone, particularly the Victorian spinster. What would the future hold? Marriage was the one career open to her: but time was racing away.

In the middle of May the family went to the Isle of Wight, to lodgings in Carisbrooke House, Madeira Road, Ventnor. Whatever travel plans they had originally had for that summer had to be shelved. John Forster Baird was seriously ill. At the beginning of June he developed congestion of the lung and pleurisy. Abroad was out of the question, and the Teddington doctor advised a holiday away from the Thames Valley. The Isle of Wight was well known for its balmy climate, 'almost Italian in its mildness', according to Baedeker's *London and its Environs*, and it was much in the news (the Queen, Tennyson and Karl Marx were among its more distinguished visitors). It would be a good place for him – for them all – to recover.

'I suppose it is nice here,' was Mary's grudging comment at the start of their stay. Carisbrooke House was a walk away from the sea, but only the children were able to benefit from it. Their mother, now nearly six months pregnant, could get down the hills but the return journey up was a trial, and their father was so weakened by his chest complaint that it was a good month before he could even go out into the garden. Most of the time he lay on a sofa being looked after by a succession of nurses. Mary wrote to Mr Trinder to have him prayed for in Teddington, as he was in the local Ventnor church. 'Poor Papa is terribly weak and nervous,' she wrote, 'his face pinched and grey and his eyes and nose have the peculiar and dreadful look that shocked me so in poor Uncle William a fortnight before his death.' (Images from the recent family deaths haunted the girls: Emmie, visiting a poor two-year-old who lived near by, 'with a white little face . . . and big blue saucer-like eyes', was reminded of Gertrude two months earlier.) The local doctor said the patient's heart was affected. The holiday, meant to last two weeks, stretched to ten.

It was bad luck they struck one of the hottest summers ever. The Bairds borrowed the shady garden of a friendly couple next door, and there was always the seashore and the sea itself for relief ('it is so lovely to feel oneself cleaving the cool clear waters', wrote Emmie). But Mary felt imprisoned, by place and people. The aunts came to stay: Auntie Jane and Aunt Frank, both very concerned about their ill brother. The family was tightly packed in their not so roomy lodgings and lacked the leaven of their normal Teddington circle.

There was a lot of work to do preparing for the new baby, 'Bacon' as s/he was bizarrely known. Mary hoped it would be 'a true "son of consolation"', adding: 'I would for my part prefer "a daughter of consolation"' (she got her wish). But her immediate grief, a focus for the larger sense of loss that underlaid all her and Emmie's diary entries at this point, was her separation from the Sunday school classes. Suddenly they seemed like the greatest blessing in her life, her one raison d'être.

Wrenched away from her Teddington life, in a strange environment, she clearly felt her sense of identity crumbling. She had broken off her engagement to Jerry at the end of the previous year. Scarcely recovered from that, she'd faced the shattering loss of Gertrude's death. Then, two weeks after they left Teddington, the Isle of Wight doctor's verdict was that her father should never risk wintering there again. Her parents began discussing giving up Woodlands for good.

Mary's morale plummeted. 'I feel often that dreadful sensation of "being alone on a hill" – alone, alone – that word expresses it – what shall I do through all the years I may have to live? People in books "find Jesus", and then are quite indifferent to all earth's miseries – why cannot I "find" Him and be happy too? I make resolutions, and say my prayers well one day, then the next I wake up late and cannot find time, and all goes cross, and I feel hopeless.

What shall I do?' Misery made its mark: she developed boils, one on each arm. Sepsis stalked the family again.

Then, three days later, the clouds miraculously began to clear: 'I *am* happier tonight, oh so much happier.' She was not sure whether the source of her happiness was because she had "found Jesus"; what was incontrovertible was that the agents handling their lease of the Teddington house had written to say that they would pay for half the alterations. Evidently the decision to move was tied up with changes needed in the house. Money, not health, had been the problem, or a major part of it. The risk of moving now receded. 'We may be able to return to the home I love so much, the scene of the happiest years of my life.'

Charting these ups and downs in Mary's mood you feel that she, of them all, was the most at sea during those weeks away. Some inner anchor, some hope or focus had vanished in the aftermath of Gertrude's death. Mary had always taken herself, all her feelings and doings very, very seriously. You can call this ego, personality or plain selfishness. It was a quality which in good times gave her her irresistible zest, in bad times her self-chastising discontent. Zest, in the days after the estate agent's letter, was now beginning to shine through.

Ventnor, meanwhile, was living up to its reputation as a place of healing. Mary's boils were on the mend. By mid-July, John Forster Baird's condition had begun to improve. As he started to take small walks around the garden, the family could imagine life returning to normal, a different and truncated normal, it was true, but one with the excitement of an imminent addition to the family.

A family argument developed around when they should they go back. The scene is only too easy to imagine. Nobody had quite enough to do, a baby was looming (the girls, as before, did not know quite when – to judge by their mother's heavy gait it

must be soon), but their father was still convalescent. Too early
a return to the miasmic Thames valley might be a disaster, too
late and the baby might arrive in the wrong place. In quiet
Emmie's view, Mary's desire to go back to Teddington reached
'mania' proportions, but their mother would not leave till she
was sure her husband was well enough to follow soon afterwards.
Result: impasse.

Even Emmie's tolerance was tested ('I don't think Mary ought
really to give way to wretchedness because we can't go home yet;
of course it *is* dull here . . . yet she ought to resign herself to the
inevitable, and forget her own wishes, or try to do so, for the good
of others – I don't practise, I fear, what I preach,' she added). But
Emmie had worked out her own way of dealing with this anxious
limbo they found themselves in. She had applied herself to
teaching and playing with the younger sisters ('my children' as she
protectively called them). Down on the beach they built sand
castles and made up Gertrude-ish stories about mediaeval ladies
and their absent loves. Back in their lodgings she read aloud:
psalms with her parents and *The Heir of Redclyffe* with her sisters
(this last having the advantage of being 'a Sunday book' as well,
i.e. one that unlike some was allowed to be read, by puritanical
Mama presumably, on Sundays).

Then, suddenly, the homecoming problem was resolved by
Auntie Jane. Auntie Jane would travel back early with Mary, who
would then stay with their Teddington neighbours, the Bartons,
till the rest of the family returned. That way she would be back
in time for her summer outing with the Sunday school girls.

Sun follows shade in Mary's diary with startling speed and no
awareness of inconsistency. One minute she is worrying about
a scene with her mother: 'At breakfast everybody's remarks seem
to go against the grain, *my* grain, I mean. . . . Mama says how
disagreeable I am, which is usually true, but oh! how I wish I

had not got alienated from my mother. . . . I have never cried so much in my life as I have during this past month.' The next she is contemplating 'the bliss (I can use no other word) of seeing home and the faces I love so much'.

And then there came an unexpected moment of laughter such as the family had not experienced for months. They were talking about going abroad, and their mother said 'she felt as if between now and then there was a great gulf fixed, beyond which her imagination could not soar', a remark that sent them all into peals of laughter. It does not seem a very funny now (humour rarely translates across the ages), but the image sparked something, or perhaps it was just the relief of being able to discuss the future again and travel, that life-blood of the Bairds (and this time their father had been ordered abroad). They sat round the supper table, lightened by their mother's joky reference to her approaching confinement and revelling in the sudden unexpected burst of laughter it had triggered; a reclaiming of happiness after the months of grief.

Two days later Mary went home, accompanied by Auntie Jane; the others to follow within a week. Woodlands was being prepared by the servants. Emmie received a 'nice bright letter' from Mary – a new, restored-to-life Mary – telling them 'it all looked very nice'. Emmie's only negative thoughts as she faced leaving Ventnor were regret for the bathing and a fear of what home would feel like without Gertrude. But Louisa was expected the next weekend; their first three months' mourning would end with the emotional catharsis of her visit which would leave them all damp-eyed, with spirits soothed.

Those days when Mary was alone in Teddington before the rest of the family joined her were crucial for her. She was staying with the Bartons, about whom we know nothing except that Jack had squired her to the Boat Race and his parents were evidently easy hosts. She slipped back into her Teddington life: the Sunday school outing to the Crystal Palace with her bunch of eight pupils, tea with the Burchells (no Jerry present), a visit to Gertrude's grave where she cut the grass with scissors, followed by a very pleasant Sunday which in her words 'opened a page of my history which I thought was long ago closed for ever'. Who did she see in church that morning (in 'the Rhodes' pew'), whose voice ('which has haunted me so long') did she hear behind her as she walked home after the service? The 'inflammable' Mortimer was on the scene again. (We know nothing about this character beyond this nickname which the two eldest girls used for him. Briefly enamoured of Mary, he had passed through Teddington a couple of years earlier. Now he was back again, the guest of their neighbour, Mrs Rhodes.)

They met at church, at tea, at supper. Mary and he sat in the Bartons' garden discussing 'the greenness of the grass', they talked about astronomy on the way to Evensong and at supper they 'astronomized' again. After supper, while Mrs Rhodes played hymns, 'we sat on the sofa and he fanned me &c &c.' Mary's diary is full of '&cs' at this point.

She was left 'very much excited and extremely puzzled'. Would it ever have an end, she asked herself, 'it' being the emotional entanglements she attracted like a magnet. 'But I *won't, won't, won't* fall in love with him yet, or get myself into another mess.' Mrs Rhodes was going away, so Mortimer too was leaving; there would be peace for a time at least. 'Do I want peace though?' Mary asked. (Her honesty is like flashes of lightning illuminating her introspections.) No, of course she did not want peace. This sort of thing was the stuff of life for her. Mortimer was exactly what the doctor ordered: her heart beat faster, she had found a new beau; even the confusion (I-love-him, I-love-him-not) was therapeutic.

Her cousin Savile Crossley, meanwhile, was rumoured to be engaged. Mary 'fumed about all day' when she heard (she was nothing if not human), but two days later had come to her senses. She just wanted him, her special confidant, to tell her himself: 'Savile is a darling boy, and I could never have him myself, so why should I grudge him little Florence Bagley?' (Little Florence, however, did not last long. Within four months the engagement was broken off, causing much distress to the Bagley family who then proceeded to vilify the Crossleys, to Aunt Frank's and everybody's embarrassment.)

The aunts were still anxious about their brother-in-law, not to mention their expectant sister. Aunt Broome came to stay, a visit that coincided with the weather breaking and a colossal thunderstorm one night during which she cowered in a corner of her room with a bolster over her head and the pregnant Emily, coming in to see if she was all right, tripped over her hip-bath in the dark. The two Brinton sisters were unscathed, but Aunt Broome – perhaps because of the storm – decided she couldn't stay for the baby's birth. ('Our little brother or sister seems to be of a dawdling disposition,' commented Mary at the end of August). They had to wait another six days. Then, on September 5th, Emily had the baby after a labour of three-and-a-half hours. 'The long looked for "Bacon", the little brother, is a sister after all,' wrote Mary happily. She had hoped for a 'soft little new Doty', and here she was, unnamed as of yet (in fact her names, Margaret Agatha, were only decided on the way to the christening five weeks later), but she was everything Mary loved best about babies. This was the moment of détente between mother and eldest daughter. Mary became the nursery maid, a role she took on with a will ('I do so enjoy the large amount of nursing that falls to my share'); it took her mind off 'sentimental' matters. Suddenly her life was full to brim with activity – baby, visitors, teaching – which left her feeling 'worn to a thread paper', but for once this was not a complaint.

The baby's arrival seemed to symbolize the family's psychological release from mourning, the end of the first half year. A month later John Forster Baird made a brief trip north with Emmie. 'Papa seems to like to take me with him,' the latter wrote, slightly regretfully, 'perhaps it will be nice.' In fact it was, for both of them. While her father went up to the borders for shooting she stayed in Bamburgh with the Darnells. The place worked its usual magic; after a week she was writing 'I have not felt so happy for a long time.' Returning to Woodlands she was struck by her mother's slim looks: 'I wonder why having a baby always makes one look so much younger' (a surprising comment, till you remember those Victorian corsets; Emily Baird evidently worked hard to regain that 18-inch waist). Gertrude's birthday, October 4th, was remembered by Emmie in her diary with the following theological speculation: 'Doty's first birthday in Heaven – but no, they have no birthdays there. I wonder if I live to be very old, shall I . . . find her still young and bright, while I am old and grey haired? – Or will there be no difference in age in Heaven?' How could one know? It was easier to concentrate on the here and now, and Emmie's next sentence reverts to the problem of the moment: 'I fear Mary is getting too fond of Mortimer.'

Mortimer, though, whatever his real intentions, did not stand a chance. The inflammable one had never been taken that seriously by any of them; but he had served his purpose. His mere presence had brought Mary back to life; and now the Bairds were packing up to go abroad, this time for a six-month stay. They would not be back in Teddington until May of the following year, 1877.

11   The Crater's Edge

How will it end?
    Mary Baird, June 1877

Twenty people saw them off from Teddington station: nine
Trinders, two Bartons, Mary's eight Sunday school pupils and
Edith Burchell, Jerry's sister (the women of the two families had
decided to be friends again). It must have been a heart-warming
send-off for the Bairds, an enviable reminder of their place in
the community. The previous months, of course, had been
exceptional. All these people had either walked or watched the
procession down Teddington High Street on that sad April day,
all must have been concerned at John Forster Baird's ill-health,
and hardly looking forward to the gap the family's absence
would create in the life of the community. But the description
of this farewell gathering on the station platform tells you
something about Victorian life. They lived among and around
each other like members of a club in a world within a world.
Within that world there would be all grades of friendship (and
romance) and mutual caringness, and different sub-groups. It
was village life, recreated in the suburbs. This was what the Baird
children had grown up with and this was what Mary missed
when they went away.

Paris was their first stop. A Crossley cousin, Herbert, came as far as Calais with them 'for the trip' (it was very rough and everyone was sick except Emmie and the baby); there were two Darnell sisters from Bamburgh headed, like the Bairds, for Cannes, and a new nursery maid, Amelia. She must have wondered what sort of family she had landed as she sat in the train with the sprawling toddler, the big picnic basket, the breast-feeding mother (Emily was surprisingly uninhibited about this) and the chattering older children. (But Amelia proved a less than adequate baby-nurse; Mary soon took over the job and she was relegated to look after the ex-baby, Dolly.)

Another Baird migration had begun. This time the Mediterranean was their destination. They had decided to stay at Cannes for Christmas, Menton over Easter, and then have a short spell in the French Alps when the weather got warmer: a route which they were not the only seekers after health to take.

They occupied the whole of the first floor of their Cannes hotel (the Centrale), plus one room on the floor above, which gave them six bedrooms and a salon. And into the salon came other hotel guests, the Washburnes (he was American ambassador in Paris), a couple called Brodrick, a Miss Oswald and her German governess, Miss Hunnemann; another German, Fraulein Mathertuis, and Mrs Hamilton, an English widow with several children ('we are all in love with her' – Emmie). They met in the Baird salon for hymn-singing on Sunday, and on Christmas Day they all had their presents there. 'It was nice, standing by the tree . . . so like old times,' reported Emmie. And to make it more like old times the children put on a play, *The Sleeping Beauty*, in which they and their new friends took part. The Washburnes, as well as supplying three members of the cast, made the costumes, the great success of the evening, Emmie tells us, being the dragon (Miss Hunnemann): 'He was a most horrible monster, it took a good while to manufacture him: a hideous animal's mask, a body composed of a striped fur rug and green calico lining, green paws, an orange tail stuffed with hay and covered with black stripes and spots; green horns striped with silver. . . . The combat between him and Prince Pharamond [the hero, played by Lilian], was loudly encored.' An impromptu dance in Mrs Hamilton's room followed the second performance of the play (the first had been in front of the hotel servants). From Emmie's account of it one can see how Baird high-jinks could take over any place they stayed in. But to Mary (more honest, or just spoil-sport?) it was 'a time of forced gaiety with us all'. She, as always, had played the nurse, a part she hardly needed to act any more. One has a sense that as she grew up she increasingly distanced herself from family theatricals, feeling too mature or perhaps too 'holy' for them. There was a streak of the nun in her – or that was how she wanted people to see her.

All of them must have felt the forced gaiety. It was impossible to forget 'the broken chain', as she called it, – the very cause for her father's ill health, the reason for them being there. Gertrude was the unseen presence that winter. She was – had been – '"one of us,"' Mary wrote poignantly, 'as a sort of mystic idea connected itself with those words formally, as if "one of us" could not be taken.' It was harder than ever to realize the depths of their loss, the harder because by some sad yet healing process it was already becoming difficult to remember Gertrude, her look, the sound of her voice: she was spoken of as someone who '*once* lived'. This sense of losing touch with the loved departed was something that felt like a betrayal. Emmie wrote in her diary that she dreamt about Gertrude and woke with the warm sense of her presence, followed the next second by the crushing loneliness of the reality ('I could not help crying in the cold dawning'). The eldest daughters kept these feelings to themselves but seem to have understood what the other was going through. There is a gentleness in Emmie towards Mary at this time, over and above her usual tolerance.

The two were now very much the senior family, Mary seven and Emmie five years older than their next sister, Lilian. Emmie and Lilian found a drawing-teacher in Cannes and went off twice a week for lessons in watercolours. Mary meanwhile was fully occupied with the baby. She took virtually sole charge of little Margaret Agatha (not so little now, she was becoming too heavy to carry, and Mary borrowed a wicker perambulator for her). Their mother was still preoccupied with her husband's health. The local English doctor (all these Mediterranean resorts had their English doctors, for obvious reasons) told him he could only be out between ten in the morning and four in the afternoon. Apart from the occasional breast feed (continued for 'fear of greater ills', reported Mary knowingly), Emily Baird spent very little time with her youngest, leaving most of the work and care to Mary. ('Baby,' as she was called, was being weaned on to condensed milk; no wonder she was heavy.)

Mary took to the job of surrogate mother with a will, as she always had. Her love of babies was profound and based by now on a lot of experience. A naturally impatient person, she had endless patience and a special douceur with the very young which lasted all her life. As 1876 gave way to 1877 her nursery-maid duties helped to keep morbid thoughts at bay; but they would strike back in the late-at-night weekly diary entries.

Her birthday on December 3rd was always a moment for taking stock; and this year she was 21. The 'nun' holds forth: 'I can perceive no progress of any sort; the same sins grow stronger, the same faults, the same want of perseverance.' But a week later she gets nearer the heart of the matter: 'As for male society I am beginning to pine for it! here is sentiment!' And a few lines later:

'I am not unhappy now, though living in an unnatural sort of make believe happiness, as on the edge of a crater ready to burst out at any time.'

But bursting out – ideally away from the family – was not an option now. The feeling of being caged went with her when the family moved along the coast at the end of January: 'I feel myself getting out of place at home, a fearful sensation for one who knows that her whole life must be spent in the same way.' Was she talking about family life in general, or life in the Baird menage? She knew she was headed for marriage: who and when were all that had to be decided. But at this low moment when the narrowness of life in a foreign hotel reduced the family's daily routines to their lowest common denominator, she saw domesticity, withal the servants and prepared meals, as a devastatingly dreary round of petty tasks. The prospect, in any context, was not inviting, unless a hero – a Prince Pharamond – suddenly appeared on a galloping horse to slay the dragon of monotony. Heroes, as we know, were never absent for long from Mary's life.

Here is Emmie's description of her in church on her birthday: 'She and I went to St Paul's church at 8.30 this morning, it was so nice walking there together in the fresh morning air. – Oh, I have hardly ever seen my dear Mary looking so *lovely*, so sweet as today: I chanced to look at her at the 11 o'clock service (she was standing in front of me, I think it was during the Psalms) and I could hardly take my eyes away from her fair sweet face, as she stood there in her black dress, her golden hair shining from under the white frilling of her bonnet. – She looked so pure, so calm – like one imagines the saints – far lovelier now, I could not help thinking, than even in her early youth.' We know the mood Mary was in on her birthday. It is almost a shock to see her through Emmie's eyes. But from this description we can imagine the impact her physical appearance made. One glance from those blue eyes, one quick smile could be enough to ensnare an onlooker; and those Mediterranean resorts were not short of ready victims. By the time the family arrived at their next stopping point Mary was being closely watched, in and out of church, by another admirer, someone this time whose attentions she would find so disturbing only code could contain her secret feelings. Over now to Menton, for the next phase of the holiday.

The covert watcher was a certain Captain Charles Allix Griffith. Mary and Emmie secretly referred to him as 'Allix'. Mary invented a private code for the passages in her diary she felt would be dynamite if read by anyone else. (The code was easily cracked by assuming the first five words read: 'I am in love with'.) The full sentence, with code words italicized here, reads: '*I am in love with Charles Allix Griffith* and fear that *he is only flirting with me*. . . . At present I only allow myself to *admire, respect* and *pity him* – oh so much; and I might be *carried* away any day. Why are *men* such *flirts*?'

Captain Griffith was a widower; he had one lung and had come to the Mediterranean on sick leave from the army to recover, he hoped, from tuberculosis. He was very attractive. Everybody except John Foster Baird liked him; everybody felt sorry for him. Compassion, though, was known to be dangerous, a quick path to emotional entanglement, as Mary soon discovered as she spent pleasant hours chatting to him on the hotel terrace.

It is astonishing that knowingly infectious individuals like him were cruising around these holiday resorts, presumably spreading germs as they went. Even more surprisingly, the risk of infection was not one of the reasons Mary's parents gave for discouraging the romance. Nobody seemed concerned about those bacilli; not even her mother tried to haul Mary off that terrace and tell the handsome Captain – politely – to get lost. John Forster Baird certainly wanted to do that ('When Mr Griffith comes to Aix [-les-Bains] – I go!' he later exclaimed) but it was not Mary's physical health he was concerned about. In the event she did not get tuberculosis. But Mr Griffith did die of it, within less than two years. Meanwhile, Mary took several steps nearer the crater's edge.

Poor Margaret Agatha had to take a back seat. Emmie, loyally covering for her sister as stand-in au pair, described Mr Griffith in her diary: '*Very* good looking, tall and dark, with nice brown eyes, he talks so pleasantly.' She too felt sorry for him – for his bereavement, his loneliness and his cough. He would visit them in their salon in the evening after dusk strolls around the garden with Mary.

They were staying at the Hotel Bellevue, a big hotel on the western side of Menton. A painting by John Forster Baird shows the aquamarine sweep of the bay framed by pine trees with the misty mountain behind it. The family had been glad to move on from Cannes, sad to leave the new friends they had made there but looking forward to making more in Menton. This strange, shifting life, full of comings and goings, meetings and re-unions must at some level have been like life in a railway waiting-room, its sense of impermanence contributing to a suspension of normal rules. Thus the state of Captain Griffith's lungs, Mary's flouting of parental wishes, the spending of too much money (both the Cannes hotel and this one were among the most expensive in town) were things you didn't have to bother about. The state of make-believe that Mary felt she lived in seems to have been shared by them all.

And for Mary, flirting was part of it. She and Captain Griffith were both adepts. Hear Emmie's comment, on a February day of bright mistral sunshine when the rest of the family are out and she has been left, literally, holding the baby: 'I begin *seriously* to think that my sister Mary is a regular little flirt! – She was having a tête-à-tête with Admiral Gordon [another hotel resident] on the terrace nearly all morning and in the afternoon, while I minded the baby and all the rest were out on donkeys, she and Mr Griffith were talking alone in the garden till four o'clock.'

The two discussed their bereavements. There was much common ground there, his wife having died not long before Gertrude; and as the friendship developed Mary told him about Jerry. Captain Griffith's comment – 'Thank God all your life that you were saved from such a fate' – seems extreme; one wonders what she had told him about the hapless Jerry. Mary, who strangely had taken a great dislike to the captain on first meeting (was there a vanity in him that jarred?) soon decided he had an unusual capacity for enjoying life and a gift for companionship. She noted how the '*Jammer Basen*' as she called them in German ('old miseries') in the hotel had decided his life was 'not worth much'. This was just an added incentive for her; 'I *know*,' she added, 'he is a flirt of the most dangerous description', and proceeded to arrange an expedition with him (plus chaperone, we don't know who) to Monte Carlo. There they visited the Salles de Jeu, where Mary was duly shocked and fascinated by 'the calm set faces . . . dissolute looking men, side by side with painted and powdered women' (she herself never wore any make-up). They then went to a concert where they sat next to each other; both, she wrote afterwards, felt '"mesmerized" – it is the only expression I can use to describe the sensation. I think a secret chord of sympathy connects some natures'. Pasted on to a page of the diary was a dried sprig of sage with the inscription: 'Monte Carlo CAG Apl 5 1877'.

She was alive again. Baby, religious devotions, letters home – all suddenly became secondary to the Captain. As Mary Darnell, who was still holidaying with them but staying in a different hotel, sardonically put it to Emmie one Sunday, Mary was 'taken up with fulfilling her avocations in the garden'. Mary meanwhile was disturbed by the thought that the Captain might only be seeking a platonic friendship. 'Surely by this time he must have seen that I am no fit subject for such a plan.'

Her release from depression was signalled by her renewed interest in her personal appearance. A month before the Monte Carlo outing she could write: 'I hardly ever look in the glass now, and never see my back hair and glycerine my hands, or in fact take any pride in my personal appearance.' But now she and Emmie had been promoted to a 'personal allowance . . . quite a farce, of course', and had been buying new clothes: 'a pair of nice new shoes and a grey carmelite dress, both made according to my latest fads, and the latter with a view to Oxford gaieties [in the summer], but this is quite *entre nous*.' She goes on to describe her clothes, adding, 'perhaps it may interest my grandchildren – if I have any!' She and Emmie, she says, look 'rather nice on Sundays in black silks, very nicely made, but with a fussy train which is the bother of my life. I have also my black mourning cashmere altered and trimmed round the skirt with silk in which I also feel rather nice.'

We are left with a picture of the sisters, prettily elegant in their black silks as they rustle to church, Mary impatiently kicking her train out of the way, Captain Griffith waiting to eye her from the neighbouring pew. In all these goings-on Mary was obeying not only a biological imperative but a social one too. There is an illuminating passage in Emmie's diary of about the same date where she describes Mary Darnell's 'great objection to ever becoming a "spare woman" (her expression for an *old maid*. She declares she will never come abroad when she is past thirty for fear of looking like the many old maids that inhabit these coasts – I ought really soon to think about it too,' Emmie adds, 'for I am 19 years old, and everyone takes me for several years older than Mary, she looks so young.'

Mary's youthful look, which can only have been enhanced by Mr Griffith's attentions, was something that the generous Emmie took sincere pleasure in. Whatever she said about her own age, it does not seem to have bothered her greatly; Mary Darnell's concerns rather amused her. Perhaps the key to the success of the Baird girls – in the Victorian marriage-market – was simply that they did not worry. And the concern of their parents was less to encourage suitors than, at this stage at least, to bat them away.

This, too, was part of the spice of it all for Mary. 'Emmie and Papa are in Rome, and I am pretty happy just now; in fact *very* – but I know there will be a row when they come back, and *he* [father] sees the progress we have made in a week – oh Mary, Mary!'

But Mary was milking this whole thing for every ounce of emotion she could get out it. Captain Griffith, meanwhile, became ill (perhaps the effort he put into all that flirtation was not so good for him) and his sister arrived to nurse him. Together they took off for Italy, that great repository of all consumptives' hopes. Captain G. and the Bairds would meet again in Aix-les-Bains, their next stop (unless Papa was true to his word and removed the family to prevent a meeting). Disconsolate, Mary waved goodbye as the Captain's horse-drawn omnibus lurched down the road. There was something to be pleased about that day (April 22nd): Papa had announced the renewal of the Woodlands lease, finally; but the news left Mary cold. 'How strangely our minds are made: the pleasures that we covet and anticipate need only to come within our reach – to prove themselves disappointing will-o' the wisps.' She might philosophize in her journal, but it did not make her feel any better.

She suffered a bad attack of '*Sehnsucht*', or longing (it sounded better in German). And meanwhile they were packing up for the next move; again, newly laid down roots were to be torn up. The whole family had liked Menton ('I have become quite attached to this smug little Menton' – Mary), with its old-fashioned houses and busy single paved street curving round the harbour. The other, eastern, bay would have been a better place to stay, Mary had thought at the beginning, better for robust people, she said, forgetting that the family was a little less than robust now (and who would have been her Mr Griffith then, one wonders). In fact it was a small enough resort for most of the English visitors to meet each other, either at church or in the main street. One such visitor the Bairds bumped into was Savile Crossley's discarded fiancée, 'little' Florence Bagley. She cut Mary and Emmie dead, and both she and Mary went very red, Emmie reported. Mary was corresponding with Savile at this time, having resumed her role of confidant. Savile, as she knew, was planning her and Emmie's visit to Oxford for Commem week in June, for which, as we've seen, she had bought the grey carmelite dress.

They had a tedious journey up to Aix-les-Bains via a night in Turin. There was trouble with the customs at Ventimiglia and again at Modane on the French border. Going through the Mont Cenis tunnel Mary nursed the sleeping baby, morbidly imagining the family getting crushed under the mountain. Describing the state of fatigue and general unsettledness they all felt when they finally arrived in Aix she finds six words for it: her mother is cross, Emmie aggrieved, Lilian vexed, Dolly quarrelsome, the baby squalling and she herself dispirited and cross as well. Only John Forster Baird was left out of this list. He was probably off on a quiet walk, checking out the views. The very next day, in a private act of homage to familiar scenery and the reassuring permanences of nature, he did a watercolour painting of the distant snow-covered Savoy mountains.

Meanwhile their hotel (the Hôtel de l'Europe) had muddled their booking. They were farmed out into an annex, then a few days later given a chalet in the grounds. Here they established themselves, making yet another home; their meals were in the hotel which meant a walk through the garden, but in their chalet they had what amounted to their own house. On the first-floor balcony under the carved wooden beams, Emmie would hold her classes in sewing and reading with the younger children, while Mary returned to baby-minding. Aix was a 'damp little rainy spot', but it had its compensations. The wild flowers and views, when you could see them, were spectacular; Mary compared the tree-covered mountains with the velvety bloom on ripe plums. There was a comfortable lushness in this landscape compared with the hot Mediterranean; their parents had always preferred this type of scenery, and for Mary life in the chalet meant liberation. She had her own room for the first time since Cannes – no more sharing with the little ones. They were only going to be there a month, but the family were getting back to their old continental routine – a sign of John Forster Baird's restored health – of mountain walks, picnics and relaxed family evenings. The anniversary of Gertrude's death, April 29th, a Sunday, was celebrated by singing the hymns they had had at her funeral. The year of mourning was over. Black mourning-dress would be with them until they got home, but home was now drawing near. Both Emmie and Mary confided to their journals how much they were looking forward to their own rooms at Woodlands. The little chalet rooms were a reminder of what they missed.

Into the middle of this last act of the family holiday came Captain Griffith. He had written to John Forster Baird, telling him he had a slight cough and increased difficulty breathing, news which can hardly have ingratiated him to his would-be host. But John Forster Baird did not leave; he confined himself to 'fuming' (Emmie's word) as he sat behind Mary and the intruding suitor in church. And the latter, perhaps feeling that time was not on his side, stepped up the pace of his apparent courtship. On an afternoon walk (when they'd managed to shake off a younger sister) Mr Griffith barred Mary's way across a plank which spanned a stream, refusing to let her pass unless she kissed him, which she did (recorded in code in the diary). The incident left her 'in a dreadful state of rage . . . but *it was so nice*'.

A day later the Bairds were on their way to Paris. Promises had been exchanged: Mr Griffith could visit them in Teddington, Mary would send him her photograph. She had her photo taken in the Champs-Elysées, but could not decide whether to send him the spare negative: 'I have got my mouth open, and am looking so ridiculously sentimental.' In her diary she surprisingly dismisses thoughts about C.A.G. and her hopes for a summer visit from him as a 'digression'. In the excitement of Paris and approaching home, *Sehnsucht* got momentarily shelved.

The family stayed as always in or near the Rue Saint-Honoré. After they had recovered from the journey (their mother felt so ill a doctor had to be summoned; he ordered immediate rest and quiet), they went to the Louvre and a concert (a Mozart mass) and shopped, for the new non-mourning clothes and dress-lengths they would need when they got home. At Bon Marché

Emmie and Mary bought ready-made dresses ('it is delightful choosing ready made costumes', Emmie wrote), supposedly inexpensive, although Mary commented: 'As is generally the case with cheap shops they have turned out anything but cheap in the end.' The dresses came out of a present of 1,000 francs Papa had given them to spend, to set themselves up for the coming summer

One has the impression of money running like water through their father's fingers throughout this whole period. The Aix hotel, Emmie tell us, was (like the others they had stayed at) the most expensive in town. With no more school fees the family were now over £100 a year better off. More importantly, Great-Uncle William's legacy was making all this possible. The rationale for their luxury travel (if one were needed) was John Forster Baird's health; and it had evidently paid off – he was better.

As they all were. A psychological corner had been turned. As soon as they were back in Teddington their mother began fixing up their wardrobes (like a snake's skin change, this moment of moving out of mourning was symbolic of new beginnings). Emmie, trailing along behind her mother, struggling into last year's now out-of-date dresses and being measured for new ones, complained it was no use trying to keep up with her. Emily Baird, when not having babies or neuralgia, could be someone of exhausting energy.

There was a lot to be done, in that last week of May 1877. Mary, to be followed soon afterwards by Emmie, would be off to Oxford in a couple of weeks as the guest of Savile, who was finishing his first year at Balliol; his mother would chaperone her nieces. This scheme, thought up by the Brinton sisters, the Emily–Martha axis, was undoubtedly intended by them as the equivalent of a debutante's season, an antidote to the sort of love affairs Mary was prone to with the random 'detrimentals' (Baird-speak for louche admirers) who hung around the Mediterranean. Oxford, after all, with its large all-male population, ought to be good for a potential husband or two.

Whatever their motives – and maybe Emily Baird just wanted a break from her wayward eldest daughter – the plan was made. There was going to be a great convergence of Brintons in Oxford: Uncle John, of the carpet-mills, was bringing two of his daughters with him to the Randolph Hotel where the Baird girls would stay until Aunt Frank removed Mary and herself to the Master's Lodgings in Balliol. The Master, Dr Benjamin Jowett, had invited them to stay. Lady Crossley was an important guest. Her husband had been a baronet, a distinguished industrialist and a Member of Parliament; her son was at the college; and her son's one-time tutor, A.L. Smith, though now a don at Trinity College, had been a Balliol undergraduate whom Jowett was known to admire.

This was Mary's first taste of the Balliol connection. Its social intertwinings were a world away from the simple contours of the foreign world the Bairds had just been inhabiting. But before Mary and Emmie pack their bags and move off to this new planet, we must finish the Griffith story. The Oxford experience, much more important for Mary's future than the prospect of two giddy summer weeks might make her suspect, will wait till the next chapter.

He was as good as his word, our Mr Griffith. He turned up in Teddington in August. The girls were back from their Oxford jaunt, Mary feeling disenchanted with life at Teddington, even the Sunday school. She had been lifted out of her groove, she wrote, but had failed to find a new one. Again, 'Mama' came to the rescue. The Bairds would have a croquet and lawn-tennis party, to celebrate the newly laid tennis-court.

The party was fixed for July 19th. 'Lots of nice people are asked,' wrote Emmie, and she listed those who had already accepted, among them A.L. Smith and Mortimer, adding, 'I hope it will be nice, and not so dismally dull as lawn tennis parties usually are.' Over now to Mary: 'Thursday we have a garden party. Mortimer is coming, but – what is that to me?'

Not much; until he walked through the door. Then, ominously, 'I was not disappointed in my old opinion of L.G.M. [Mortimer], and think that had I never seen *someone else*, I might still have been fascinated by him. He has far more "*go*" than the Teddington men, and can *say things*; but I tried not to flirt with him.' A week later Mortimer was there again, but this time he had been pipped to the post by someone else. Enter Mr Griffith, and the whole thing begins to look like a Feydeau farce. Mary had both men fluttering around her: 'Whenever I was with Mr G. enjoying reminiscences and talks about old times, Mr M. buzzed about like an impatient butterfly, waiting to pounce upon me, if he didn't immediately become a third in the conversation. They *both* wanted me as a partner at lawn tennis, and *both* accompanied me round the garden on a tour of inspection undertaken at the desire of *one*. At supper circumstances willed that I should sit *between* the two, so I tried to be impartially agreeable. After supper we got up a dance, and [I] consented to sit out with both alternately – altogether a difficult business.' She 'cheered Mr Mortimer up at parting', she says, and Mr Griffith stayed the night. A week later the two men were there again, and fickle Mary notes that this time Mortimer 'was in the ascendant'. When time for church came she managed to leave Griffith at home and take Mortimer with her, ending on a note of exhaustion: 'I can't write any more except that *both* left by the 9.30 train and I have not yet heard whether anything was left of them to get to the station.' Her parents, she notes, disapprove of the two men equally.

She had got herself into a 'nice mess'. Having at first decided that neither man was serious, she now decided they both were.

It was several days before she took up her diary again, then there is one more short entry before a month's gap. On August 15th she is 'sitting in the school room alone, writing, in a thin lavender coloured print, doors and windows open, and a bright sun shining'. It is 'one of those delicious afternoons when white puffy clouds cross the sky, and all looks bright'. Life had gone back to normal. Emmie was taking four-year-old Dolly for a walk in the park; and Mary herself had started teaching Dolly: 'She comes willingly to her lessons every morning and makes pretty rapid progress, at present without any intervention from Mama, a great triumph.' All this was a relief, perhaps, from the crater's edge. But Mary would be on it again (when, in fact, had she ever been off it?)

Meanwhile, sitting in the sunlit schoolroom her thoughts could linger over the past weeks, the drama of the tennis party and before that her Oxford visit, her first stay in a place that unbeknownst to her would shape the rest of her life.

12   *Oxford*

One round of gaiety and dissipation.
Emmie's diary, June 11th 1877

The sun shone every day. From the moment the Teddington party arrived in Oxford on June 9th to the day they got home two weeks later, having done the return journey by river, the weather was perfect. Then, the very next day, it rained.

Oxford, that fine early June, was at its most magical. The college gardens were in full flower, walking about the city was a joy, so long as you stuck to the main university thoroughfares and avoided the slums of St Ebbes. On Show Sunday in Commem week everybody who was anybody paraded up and down the Broad Walk in Christchurch, the men in academic dress, their female friends and relations in their finest clothes (Mary wore her 'cream cotton' for this).

She went to three Commem balls in a row: the Trinity Commem, with Savile, Kitty Brinton and A.L. Smith on June 11th; the Masonic ball ('I wore my blue dress and had great fun') on the 12th and the Balliol ball on the 13th. (Emmie joined her for the last two.) Then as now a Commem ball meant dancing all night, breakfasting in the pearly grey dawn and, for Mary after the last two, letting herself into the Master's lodgings at Balliol with her own latch-key as the sun rose. There is a photograph of the Baird–Brinton party on the lawn at Trinity in the middle of this strenuous week. Not surprisingly, they look a jaded bunch. Savile, astride a chair on the left, is propping his head on one bent arm, likewise Mary, standing in the middle of the back row – A.L. Smith had to escort her back to the Randolph after this, she felt so 'knocked up'. A.L. himself sits on the grass at Emmie's feet. Both have a look of stoned abstraction, though for Emmie this was a moment of rare delight. She had travelled up to Oxford with A.L. and 'hardly ever enjoyed myself so much' (poor Emmie, those modest heart-strings were beginning to twang). Only Aunt Frank, next to Mary, is composed enough to remember to turn her profile – her 'good side' – to the camera. It is a neap point in a giddy week.

The other four men were friends mustered by Savile and A.L. as escorts for the lady cousins. Mary lists their names, and others she met. There was a character called Rodd (the future Lord James Rennell Rodd), one Portal (later Sir Gerald, diplomat), a Wickens (son of Sir John W., barrister and Old Etonian). These were the products of the public school system, the cream of the upper and upper-middle classes. To them university was a continuation of school, but with more play and a keener level of intellectual diversion, if desired. Rowy Mitchison (another of Mary's granddaughters) summed up their university role: 'These young men came up at nineteen to a limited but enjoyable and protected existence in which those with a natural bent for scholarship could experience it, and those not so afflicted were unembarrassed by its absence.'

This is not to say that all or even any of those nameless young men in the Trinity garden photograph fell into that last category. A.L. Smith was collecting around him friends who shared his academic ideals of wider opportunity and greater academic rigour. And there was a very different kind of university life emerging, a world within a world whose influence was beginning to spread and capture minds in a way similar to the fervour with which the Oxford movement had burst on the city 30 years earlier. This was the new scholarship, a growing commitment to higher educational standards, mirroring the national mood. Out of this had come a reassessment of the role of the country's oldest universities. In the vanguard of this questioning was A.L.'s ally, the 51-year-old Benjamin Jowett. Though a lifelong classicist himself, Jowett's dream was to broaden the university to include science, mathematics and more liberal arts, and to widen its social intake. 'At present not a tenth or twentieth part of the ability of the country comes to the University' Jowett had noted, and he saw this as an incalculable loss to the nation. To rectify this meant, among other things, dropping the celibacy rule for college fellows, unchanged since the Middle Ages, which was driving young teaching talent away.

In fact the moment the Baird–Crossley crowd chose for their visit was a crucial one for Oxford. The Royal Commission on the universities had been meeting that year. Out of this was to come the Universities of Oxford and Cambridge Act, leading to more democratic college government, adjustments to university finances which would make possible the development of new subjects and, of utmost importance to Mary's future, the abandonment of the ancient celibacy rule.

But as they sat in the college gardens and composed themselves for the photograph, our visitors knew nothing of this. Nor did their escorts, except for A.L. Smith (who shared many of Jowett's ideas) and perhaps some of his academic colleagues. A.L. was a Fellow of Trinity then, but he was also studying law as a surer route to a career, given that an Oxford fellowship would bar him from marriage. His hollow-eyed stare might have been the result not just of the all-night Trinity ball but of juggling two careers, taking on simultaneous teaching and learning responsibilities.

A.L. had introduced some of his senior common room fellows to the Bairds. Mary in fact was being exposed to university life at all levels. When she and her aunt moved to the Master's Lodgings as guests of Jowett, their fellow guests were Lord and Lady Coleridge, he the future Lord Chief Justice of England who was in Oxford to receive an honorary degree at the annual encaenia (degree-giving ceremony) in the Sheldonian. To that great tribal display of academia the whole party trooped the next day, and after the ceremony there was lunch at All Souls where Mary was conducted into the Codrington Library by Jowett himself.

This was another moment when a friendly angel might have descended with a helpful message, this time to Mary ('Oxford will be your world, your lair, for the rest of your life'). But as she entered that elegant 18th-century building on Jowett's arm, our irreverent young lady was not impressed. At Balliol she had felt back-achey and bored, and dinner there with all the nobs had been 'very dull'. Here too, the All Souls lunch, though 'an improving occasion', was dismissed in her diary as 'dull'. We know from Jowett's commonplace book that among the people he was in touch with that summer were George Eliot, Tennyson and Florence Nightingale (who was one of his closest friends). If Mary had been able to tap into his world, or if she had known that that kindly, if intimidating, man was one day going to pay, out of his own pocket, for a house (the King's Mound) to be built on Balliol ground for her and her future family, she might have found the occasion a little less dispiriting.

That afternoon, fatigue notwithstanding, she went on from All Souls to a fête in Worcester College gardens which evoked this telling comment in her diary: 'Great fun, as I got rid of the swells.'

She was developing a deeply ingrained 'anti-swell' streak. Where did it come from, and why was it such a lasting characteristic? Her own husband would become a swell, and most of her daughters' husbands too, but she handed this social iconoclasty down to more than one of them. During this first visit of hers to Oxford it could be seen as an instinctively defensive reaction in a bright but eccentrically educated young woman to the company of her more cultivated peers, or alternatively as the healthy response of someone whose natural intelligence made them quick to detect humbug and pomposity. Whatever its roots, this fighting soul of hers became Mary's hallmark, and later her salvation. From it she drew the strength needed for the challenges in her life: the raising of a large family, setting up and running baby clinics, and presiding over an ever shifting social empire.

After their round of Oxford gaiety, on Thursday June 14th the second part of the holiday began. Breakfast in A.L.'s rooms was followed by a party of nine of them going down to the Balliol boathouse on the Thames, where two rowing-boats, double scullers, were waiting for them to board. Jowett saw them off. After the picnic hamper and luggage had been loaded, the men got into the rowing seats. A.L. and Savile were in one boat, Wicken and Rodd in the other, with Aunt Frank, Kitty and Emmie in the first and Mary and Annie ('Savile's Annie' Mary calls her – we know nothing more about her than that) in the second. And off they set.

It was a journey to Teddington (by river) of just over 93 miles, spread over seven days. The men were good rowers. A.L. had been in the Balliol Eight when he was an undergraduate and wanted to keep up his rowing, so this daily stint at the oars would have been sheer pleasure for him. The prize for endurance, though, must surely go to Aunt Frank. Look again at that Trinity gardens photo. Those were the kind of clothes she got into the boat in, that high bonnet with its flowing ribbons perched on her careful chignon. The dress would have had a tight waist, and under it she would have been buttressed by a whalebone corset. Into that boat, morning after morning and afternoon after afternoon she was handed, to sit there and be splashed by the oars, scrambled over at the locks and feel (Mary noted this) mounting disapproval at the 'ballyragging' of the youngsters and their sometimes raucous singing when they shipped oars (more water dripping on to her skirt) and drifted down the stream.

The photograph album with the Oxford picture also has pictures of the river trip (all save one of riverscapes; the only one with figures shows two people in a boat, looking suspiciously like A.L. and Savile, with Windsor Castle in the background, captioned 'HRH the P—ce of W—s' and 'Sir S. C——y, not yet adult'). The threepenny lock tickets (one was required for each person) have been painstakingly glued in the album, also the spoof dance programmes for their evening hops at the inns they stopped at. 'Miss B.' someone has pencilled in for dances one to twelve, followed by 'supper', presumably in A.L's handwriting; but, Mary tells us in her diary: 'I had no especial favourite!!!' – the three exclamation marks denoting her surprise at herself.

In this holiday atmosphere there was too much fun, and they were living too close to each other for the excludingness of flirtation to be tempting. They sang, they laughed, they recited (and wrote) poetry, and when Aunt Frank had been deposited at their evening stopping point they tied the boats together and sculled silently through the dark under the winking stars, returning just before midnight ('Aunt F *rather* cross'); and on

Sunday they warbled river versions of hymns which surely would have shocked their chaperone. Emmie's and Mary's diaries capture the atmosphere of freedom of that week, and the batty almost incomprehensible poems pasted in the album give you the feeling of a group of young people who have virtually reverted to childhood (at Medmenham Abbey they ran around the ruins pretending to be ghosts). Perhaps, notwithstanding its excitements, that visit to Oxford had been oppressive for all of them, not just Mary. At their last stop, at the Swan Inn in Staines, they 'laughed so much at supper that we could hardly stop', reported Emmie, then played blindman's buff and finished up with a sing-song. After an 18-mile row the next day they were back in Teddington.

A new side of Mary was emerging. She was lustily joining in all the group's entertainment – witness her entry for June 18th: 'Got out at Marlow to "liquor up".' When she helped to roll up the dusty carpet at the Roebuck Inn at Mapledurham after a picnic lunch trespassing in Streatley Woods, she was reclaiming a part of her youth that had got buried during those years and months of bereavement and obsessive flirtation. And it had a curiously stabilizing effect. Just as the pious Sunday school teacher had been left behind at Teddington, never quite to be retrieved, so the insecure and self-doubting flirt was being replaced by someone with greater self-assurance. Her lambent high spirits still shone, but with a steadier glow.

The next lap of the summer took the whole family to Bamburgh. The servants could get on with cleaning the Teddington house, John Forster Baird could enjoy his bloodsports on the borders and sketching on the beach, the baby would benefit from the sea air (she had already had some mysterious fevers which mystified the doctor and terrified her parents). So off they went for yet another month-long stay in

Wynding House, to be met at Belford station by Willie Dixon and his horse-drawn cart. And this year the party included Savile and A.L. Smith.

Play became the order of the day, boyish outdoor exploits which place and good weather conspired to promote ('excursionizing, crabbing, shrimping, boating etc. – and fancy dress balls at night, charades and all kinds of fun', recorded Emmie). When Mary tired of these exertions there were still 'the babies' to tend. Her new maturity had not dented her love for the very young; the gradual unfolding of Dolly's mind, under her tutelage, was a continual source of delight to her.

So much so that when it was mooted that she, Mary, should return with 'the boys' (A.L. and Savile) to Somerleyton after only two weeks at Bamburgh, she rebelled. It's hard, trying to read between the lines of her account and Emmie's, to see what exactly was going on. According to Emmie it was during this Bamburgh holiday that John Forster Baird conceived a great dislike of A.L. Smith. We shall see more of this antagonism in the next chapter; here it's enough to note Emmie's comment, and wonder whether her father was not perhaps an unconscious barometer of change, like a piece of seaweed in the hall, his hostility registering the new focus in A.L.'s attentions. But while her father was bristling, her mother it seems was doing her utmost to throw Mary and A.L. together; why else did she decide Mary should go to Somerleyton? It begins to look like another Brinton conspiracy, and perhaps that too contributed to John Forster Baird's irritation, a sense of being outmanoeuvred by his scheming womenfolk.

Mary, aware of the tension in her father, indeed feeling upset that yet another Bamburgh holiday was being soured by bad relations with her parents, dropped her resistance to leaving. 'I get on so badly with both Papa and Mama (grieved and ashamed as I am to write this) perhaps absence in this case will make the heart grow fonder. But I [shall] miss our sweet baby, now just a year old, and Dolly and Emmie and all.' She wrote as if she was preparing herself for exile.

Yet when the crater opened in front of her, it was a total surprise. That at least is what she wanted others to believe. If she was deceiving anybody, it was surely herself. She and the 27-year-old A.L. had been to three balls together, they had danced on dusty inn floors, they had joked and played hide-and-seek in abbey ruins and she had watched his athletic arms pulling the oars for 90 miles of summer river, seen those authoritative eyes measuring the distance as they approached the locks (he, as the senior man in the group, would have been in charge of that river trip). But – and it is an important but – they had known each other for years. He had seen her in Jerry-mode (for Jerry read Mortimer/Griffiths/whoever) and she had seen him year in year out as the protégé of a rich aunt with the lowly status of tutor, the serious academic who was employed to get her amiable cousin into Oxford.

The transition from being part of the landscape to taking centre stage can happen in a trice. The prelude could have been a squeeze of the hand, a word. The receiver – or viewer – just has to be ready; and Mary most certainly was. In this case the moment is recorded in her diary. It was a look.

It happened on the third day of her stay at Somerleyton. They had arrived on September 12th. The Crossley menage, in spite of its austere Sundays, seemed luxurious after Bamburgh. There were no sisters for her to have to bother about, an indulgent aunt in place of critical mother, she was one lone girl among three 'boys', as she called them (Savile had an Etonian friend to stay). It was a time of river trips, evening dances and strolls in the winter garden. Then, on day three of her visit, everything changed.

She and A.L. had what she calls a 'trial of strength'. Her diary entry for the day reads as follows:

I am afraid I am on the verge of a serious entanglement, and that with the said individual [A.L.] whom I considered a safe person. I don't know what has come over him; his conduct is most eccentric. . . . He is continually in my company, wasting his time most shamefully – Oh Mary, Mary, if I were only an outside confidante to advise you I would tell you how much danger you run into by being too yielding, and yet not exactly that, for I have had a trial of strength with him this morning about something he wanted me to do, and came out of it victorious. Yet somehow I couldn't triumph, for as he yielded the point his face fell and he said, looking down with an expression I could not understand, 'You will always get it.' I was so puzzled that I began to feel quite uncomfortable and came upstairs, to my room, where I am writing now – hoping that he will have time to recover himself. I quite dread meeting him at lunch.

A.L. Smith had none of the social skills of a Charles Griffith, none of his accomplished flirtatiousness. He had a habit of hiding his feelings under a veneer of flippancy which Mary found offputting. But with that downcast look a seriousness and vulnerability suddenly showed which she had probably never encountered in her flirtatious life before; and it put her in a spin.

The transition from family friend to prospective lover was not easy for her to adjust to. She does not understand him or his feelings, she says, and as for her own – she writes three lines then scratches them out later. The mere fact that she was so keen no one should read them, however, makes it easy to imagine the kind of hostile comment they might contain; or perhaps they were an expression of panic, a silent Iphigenia-like scream of a young girl who had come face to face with what she knew was, at last, the real thing.

But the spell had been cast. A.L. dropped his bantering manner and started treating her like an equal. This involved a lot of serious talk: 'A.L.S. has taken up improving my poor little mind. I fear he will find it hard and unprofitable labour!' But she listened as he (too) astronomized, then turned a readier ear when he began to tell her about his own background, which could not have been more different from her own. There seems to have been a Crossley conspiracy to leave them together. They dined alone, the others having been conveniently invited out, then walked in the winter garden with an oil lamp, picking flowers for each other. This should have seemed more like real romance for Mary (remembering that sprig of sage at Monte Carlo), but her comment now, 'Oh, why am I such an idiot – and is this the way a learned Oxford Don behaves!' shows either that A.L. lacked Mr G.'s style, or that Mary's expectation had changed. Both were probably true. Playing at love was no longer what she wanted.

On September 21st she felt herself standing on the edge of a precipice. A.L., she writes, is a hard case: 'He is so very persistent.' Four days later she announces, 'I believe the right thing has come to me at last – the strong pure love of a true man.' She still does not quite know what she feels and asks with devastating honesty: 'Is this intense thrill that pervades me only that of gratified vanity? I know myself too ill to say.'

The previous evening they had had a long talk. The scene again was the winter garden. What exactly was said between them even the diary cannot be told. 'Somehow his words seem too sacred to repeat. I have never known such intense feeling before. . . . My whole frame trembled.' A.L., indirect as usual, asked Mary to promise him she would not throw him over. 'Taking both my hands [he] desired me to promise this; but I hesitated, feeling somehow as if a great deal was involved in it. Was it gratified vanity, or was it "the real thing" that made me grant it at last? He then stooped and kissed my right hand, which he was holding, as if a solemn compact were ratified by so doing, and I, as soon as I had recovered, went into the dining hall where all were sitting, looking, I believe, as white as a sheet.' She still didn't really know what his intentions were. The day's entry ends in confusion: 'I can safely say that I have never heard anything but good of him – and – Oh Mary, Mary!', and she stops in mid-phrase.

'Mary, Mary!' is her private *cri-de-cœur*, a gathering up of the corners of herself as she tries to keep her inner poise. In the days that followed she felt that he was drifting down the stream, while she was being carried along by his passion. A.L. was a man of great physical as well as intellectual energy, and Mary's diary encapsulates the charged atmosphere of those days, with A.L. fixed on his wooing and she unable not to respond to it. Savile and his mother were the sympathetic onlookers: their role in this whole business would be of crucial importance later on. Meanwhile a pragmatic note entered Mary's musings: 'If it is true, as I believe, CAG [Mr Griffith] is only a flirt, there can be no harm in my transferring my affections to one whom I know to be in real earnest.' In other words, you waited to be loved, weighed up the value of the proffered package, then released the wellsprings of devotion in yourself. A.L. was the less sophisticated but infinitely the more serious and the more romantic of the two men. (After their engagement he lent her a copy of William Morris's 'Earthly Paradise', a favourite poem of his, which has these lines: 'Look up, love! – ah, cling close and never move!/How can I have enough of life and love?') Between the lines of Mary's diary you glimpse a man whose dedication to life and love has found its apotheosis in his commitment to her.

The day of her return to Teddington came. The house party, which by then included uncle John Brinton and his wife Mary, left by train to London, A.L. and Mary in her uncle's compartment, a journey that was 'great fun, especially when the elders were asleep'. A.L. accompanied Mary to Waterloo ('I could hardly manage him in the cab'); then it was home to Woodlands, back to the Sunday school routine and parents who clearly scented something was up (what had the letters from Somerleyton said?). John Forster Baird seized every opportunity to disparage A.L. He was becoming more primitive with age – age and illness and possibly financial worries. His sketches from this period have a shakiness about them which suggest creeping ill-health. While sympathizing with Mary it is impossible not to feel a pang for this talented, unambitious father of hers. In A.L. Smith he had come face to face with a new kind of being who had been honed by the spirit of a very different age from the one he himself had been born into.

The denouement came five days later. On Sunday October 21st A.L. arrived in Teddington, late for lunch after he'd walked from South Kensington ('Mary turned first red then pale,' wrote Emmie). He spent the afternoon closeted with their mother while Mary was in Sunday school. Emily Baird then spoke to her husband. The upshot was that A.L. was not given permission to address Mary (her mother had told him he wouldn't have a chance with her, anyway). As if to underline this Mr Griffith appeared, as charming as ever and apparently in better health, though still coughing. The two admirers, to the girls' surprise, warmed to each other. They left together at the end of the afternoon (in fact Mr G. spent the night in A.L.'s lodgings). To Mr Griffith the latter was, anyway, 'Emmie's Mr Smith', a misapprehension which Mary for the moment did nothing to dispel.

Her parents' obduracy only strengthened Mary's resolve. 'Can I trust you?' A.L. wrote in a book under cover of the Sunday evening hymn-singing before he left, Mary whispering a heartfelt 'Yes!' After all, parents' opposition was part of the drama. She finally brought Emmie into her secret, which gave her an ally in the family. Emmie, loyal to the core, forgot any earlier fantasies she might have nursed and told A.L. she would 'always take Mary's part'.

Somerleyton now entered the scene. Something momentous (one imagines a stream of Crossley–Baird letters) happened between Sunday 21st and Wednesday 24th. By Wednesday evening, John Forster Baird had retreated: A.L. could come the following day to ask formally for Mary's hand. And on Thursday permission was granted, but there would be no public engagement until 'Arthur [for the first time in her diary Mary calls him this] has a good appointment and sufficient income'. But 'having secured me he is going up to Oxford to make arrangements . . . all will be smooth. The family's objections have all vanished into thin air, and I feel so happy, if only he were here.' Thus it was decided; and thus ends Mary's diary.

There was another letter, which had perhaps helped swing matters as well as the pressure from Somerleyton. Two days earlier A.L. had written to John Forster Baird, as follows:

9 Alfred Place, S. Kensington 22 Oct 1877

Dear Mr Baird,

In my desire to justify your and Mrs Baird's kindness to me and (as I imagined) good opinion of me, I took the unusual course of speaking to her before getting a verdict, whether favourable or the reverse, from your daughter. And I trust that you will be quite open with me and as considerate as you can, that I may have no reason to regret this course. Mrs Baird will do me the justice to allow that I am disposed to submit to your wishes; and only claim, in justice to your daughter as well as to myself, the right to receive her part of the decision from her mouth. Should this be one favourable to me, I fully acknowledge still your right to impose what terms precedent you please; to say within what time I must be prepared either to come forward definitely or to give up any claim, and what permanent income I must then be able to show myself possessed of. Without grounds for confidence that I can very shortly secure this, I should not speak to you. . . .

Within the last few months I have without the slightest seeking them been offered, and in the then state of my plans refused, an assistant editorship of £500 a year, high masterships at Rugby and Clifton, and a far more promising opening which I am hardly at liberty to describe. . . .

No one can have a deeper sense of the inadequacy of anything I can offer your daughter; but I cannot assent to my prospects in the present as in the future being set down as a nonentity. But I freely admit your right of inquiry on this point; and it was precisely to admit this that I came to speak to Mrs Baird first.

Something else that was said must, I fear, have left on my mind an impression hardly intended, being an illusion to a supposed absence of religious principles. I am not given to boasting, least of all on such a topic; but I offer for inspection the whole of my life since I have grown up, I will abide by the evidence as to my conduct of anyone who has known me for any part of it; I will answer any question put to me about it. . . . I venture to think your daughter and myself would not be likely to disagree in our actions, and what weight should be attached to some supposed difference in the speculative grounds of our actions, must be left to that decision of hers by which I am to abide. . . .

I only want to be assured of her own view. After all, it must come to that; she is grown up, is quite clear as to what her own wishes and views in general are, and is not carried away by a first inexperience. Beyond getting her present decision, I wish to leave her as free as possible in the future. I recognise the possibility of a change of mind, and would submit to it with as good a grace as possible if it came about. Believe me you would not find me exacting. . . .

But imagine yourself back in my position; and if I have said anything too much, make that allowance for it. . . . Expecting to hear when I may explain to you, and when I may get whatever answer it is to be from your daughter, I am

Yours very truly Arthur L. Smith.

This was a statement from a man putting all his cards on the table. The bantering, self-deprecatory tone which marked some of his other letters at this time had given way to stern directness. He knew his worth, and knew that Mary was aware of it too. She, as she wrote in her diary the day before he sent this letter, felt stunned with wonder at the depths and piety of his love. There was a dedicated, focused quality in him that was new to her. It was this that Mary felt awed by, and this that threatened his future father-in-law; and it was this that drove A.L. back to Oxford as soon as things were settled in Teddington to explore that 'promising opening' which would prepare the ground for his and Mary's future there.

13   *Arthur Lionel Smith*

A rough nursery.
R.H. Roe, describing Christ's Hospital

A.L.'s background was as different from Mary's as it could be. From the earliest years his childhood had been marked by bereavement and loneliness. The two people who decided in that autumn of 1877 to get married arrived at the same point in time and destiny from opposite poles.

Arthur Lionel Smith had been born in 1850, the second son of a civil engineer, William Smith, who was a native of Ireland. William Smith had come to London after the famine years and had worked with Marc Brunel (Isambard's father) on the Thames tunnel – at least that is what Mary said later. More important perhaps was William's reputed acquaintance with Sir Morton Peto, an architect and developer who was responsible for much construction work in Lowestoft and the rebuilding of Somerleyton Hall, which he later sold to the Crossleys. The intersecting circles of Victorian life suggest interesting links. Was there a professional link between Peto, the friend of the Crossleys, and William Smith the engineer, which later led to the Smith–Crossley friendship? Whatever the answer, William Smith was a talented professional in his own right. Mary owned a design of his for a floating 'flexible breakwater' for the

Goodwin sands, that shifting graveyard of sailing ships; but whether for lack of government backing or because of its inventor's death, the project came to nothing.

The Smith family lived in Red Lion Square, in the heart of London. William and his wife Alice had five children: William, Arthur, Reginald, Mary and Miriam. Reginald died from cholera as a child, probably during the 1854 outbreak in Soho, less than a mile away from Red Lion Square, which John Snow of Newcastle had mapped (thereby proving that cholera was a waterborne disease). Not long after Reginald's death their father also died, aged only 37.

The widow, with her four surviving children, could have faced destitution. But Mrs Alice Elizabeth Smith came from a highly eminent family, and though the young Smith children experienced considerable deprivation, they did not starve. Alice Elizabeth was the daughter of Jacob Strutt, a painter and engraver who had been a pupil of Constable's and whose wife was a writer. Jacob had published a book of engravings of trees, *Sylva Britannica*, in 1826. His son Arthur, Alice's brother, also a painter, regularly exhibited at the Royal Academy with his father. Both artists had gone to live in Italy where Arthur had been made a *cavaliere* by the king of Italy in recognition of his talents.

A.L. could thus be justly proud of his forebears on both sides. For Alice, his widowed mother, practical help from her family quickly followed her husband's death. Jacob and Arthur Strutt offered her a home, which she accepted. The decision to leave Holborn with its unhappy memories and to settle in sunny Italy was probably not a difficult one.

The problem, though, was the boys and their education (girls needing less, as we have seen, could be lugged around with the adults). William, the eldest son, solved matters by saying that he wanted to go into the Navy, and at that point he disappears from our story. Arthur, the third son, who had not yet at the age of six been taught to read or write (in deference, it seems, to progressive views of his father on education) was secured a presentation to Christ's Hospital through the intervention of a certain Alderman Wise. ('Here, my boy, that's worth £500. I give it to you because I knew and respected your father,' Mary reports the alderman as saying, in her life of A.L.S.) So Arthur became a bluecoat boy, a full-time boarder at Christ's Hospital. He said goodbye to his mother. He would see her once again in the next 17 years, when she visited him at school after he had had rheumatic fever.

Christ's Hospital was then in Newgate Street, in the City of London. It had been founded in the 16th century for 'the poor, the penniless and orphans' of London of either sex, but by the 19th century had become a boys-only school. In other respects it was still true to its founding principles. There were no fees, the children were given a set of clothes, the bluecoat uniform, on arrival; in fact the expression 'clothed' became synonymous with full entry to the school. Arthur was 'clothed' on February 2nd 1858, though according to school records he had been there since the previous spring, before he was six and a half. Photographs show him as a sturdy boy with a good-natured expression under thick, carefully combed hair, and a set of the jaw that became more determined as he grew older.

Another feature of this charitable institution was that homeless children could stay there all year round. Arthur, whose London home no longer existed, was one of those who did. During term time and holidays for the first six years of his life there the school was the only home he knew.

His mother wrote to him, and there was an aunt, Sarah Strutt, who certainly later was in touch and gave him some form of allowance. But in 1859 his mother remarried, to an American, Freeman Silke, and went to live in Chicago where she had another two daughters to add to the two Smith girls she took with her. Later the Silkes settled briefly in Italy in a vain fight against the consumption that afflicted Freeman. After being widowed for the second time, Alice Elizabeth made a brief visit to Arthur who was in the school infirmary with rheumatic fever, then went back to the United States for good. Arthur saw his mother twice again during his whole lifetime.

What did this do to the young boy? What effect did living in the harsh hierarchical world of boarding school have on a tender soul that had already suffered so much bereavement – brother dying of cholera (presumably at home), father dead and mother now gone away for good? The adult Arthur retained a strong affection for the school but rarely referred to his early years there. Stories survived, of the infant schoolboy having his hand closed over a glowing cinder by a senior boy when he stumbled on a word in a hymn, of having his fingers stamped on to encourage him to swim. But whatever misery he experienced, one thing seems to have come to his rescue, the message Alderman Wise had perhaps intended to convey: that education was the only way up and out of poverty, and that if you had talents you could not afford to neglect them.

Another man who had had a similar childhood and who, as we know, was to be a key figure in A.L.'s life was Benjamin Jowett. In the mid-1850s Jowett was already Regius Professor of Greek at Oxford, but a generation earlier, after poverty had chased his mother out of London, he had been left to fend for himself. The 12-year-old Benjamin had lived in lodgings and trudged his lonely way to school at St Paul's. As adults Jowett and A.L. were very different characters, the one ascetic to the point where withal his portliness he seemed to be pure intellect, the other endowed with exceptional physical energy which overflowed into a passionate love of sport as well as learning. But the two men conceived a lasting admiration for each other and shared profoundly similar views on education, forged in the same 'rough nursery'.

This phrase was used by a contemporary of A.L. at Christ's Hospital, R.H. Roe, who also went to Balliol and rowed with him in the Balliol boat. Roe's reminiscences of Christ's Hospital give a picture of a bleak place. Discipline was stern, food inadequate, sports restricted to a small asphalt playground and the curriculum divided almost equally between classics and maths. The boys were looked after by 'dames' in what were called wards, which added to the prison-like atmosphere. It was, says Roe, a hard school, but it 'tended to produce independence and strength of character and a habit of looking on the bright side of things and of doing without unnecessary luxuries'.

Was Roe thinking of his erstwhile school friend when he wrote that? All these were qualities evident in A.L. In fact Christ's Hospital was far from being a Dotheboys Hall. With all its austerity, it was notable for its nurture of the boys' intellects, and it was well organized for sport. A.L. was introduced to hockey there (in the asphalt playground), a game he conceived a lasting enthusiasm for, later producing in his own first-born child a future captain of the England hockey team; and as senior boy he was able to row in the school boat at Putney. But the greatest discovery of his first years there was books. Once over his late start, he became a voracious reader. The two main passions of his life – sport and study – were thus early on implanted in him.

The curriculum might be 50 per cent classics but classics after all was history, and history, A.L. discovered, was the door to life. My own father, meeting A.L., then Master of Balliol, soon after he, my father, had arrived there as a Rhodes Scholar after the First World War, recorded in his diary what they talked about. The two of them went for a walk along the tow-path to discuss rowing (my father rowed in the university boat). Their conversation (mainly A.L.'s, one imagines) covered 'history, physiology, the anatomy of rowing, the health and lives of oarsmen, psychology, Darwin's Origin of Species, Paradise Regained and the Russian compared to the French Revolution'. My father's comment, 'what a man, this Master of ours!' sums up the impression made by A.L.'s sweeping intellect.

His academic potential was already evident at school. His essays, 'remarkable for their compression of facts, their wide range of thought, and their sensible conclusions' (Roe), were setting him on the path to university. His tutor at the time was a certain Mr Hooper who taught classics and essay-writing to the senior boys. Under Hooper's guidance A.L. wrote a prize-winning essay which got him the offer of a classics exhibition at Balliol in November 1868. In a letter to his mother the 18-year-old assessed his future chances at the university: 'Mr Hooper says a man who gets a first rate classic (Schol.) at Oxford is made for life, and that he is certain I shall take a first. Fancy that! Is it not glorious if only true? . . . I leave you to digest that but not to be too sanguine.' A letter to his aunt Sarah Strutt focused on another side of school life: 'We are in the midst of terrific preparations for the Classical Examination. . . . I must beg of you to send me as soon as possible my allowance for June, for I have been for some time without a penny. . . . I must even borrow a couple of stamps to post this letter.'

A letter to his mother two months later is more explicit. His university exhibition will give him £40 a year for four years, plus another £40 a year from Balliol; at the end of which he would take his finals – 'upon my place in this list depends my future life'. Christ's Hospital gave all future university-goers a leaving present of £20–30 for furniture (undergraduates had to supply their own), £20 for books and £10 for clothes. This would come to a total, in his first year, of £140 followed by £80 a year for the remaining four years. Most of the rest of this letter is about ways he can try to get more money by upping his exhibition or winning essay prizes.

This was to be a constant pressure on him throughout his life: how to increase his earnings. He was at a university where the vast majority of students had private means. He not only had none, but whenever he had any cash to spare he sent it to his hard-pressed mother. The arrival of his own family of nine in the 20 years between marriage and the beginning of the next century did nothing to alleviate matters. The family's chronic low income was probably as much a factor in Mary's nunnish style of dress as her natural love of the simple and unadorned. For A.L. it was merely a continuation of life as he had always known it.

One lasting effect of this constant shortage of money was to sharpen his commitment to wider educational opportunity. His vision for his own life overlapped with his vision for society as a whole. Educational opportunity should be broadened, at the level both of the university curriculum and of extramural courses for the general public. During his London period, when wooing Mary, he was teaching evening classes to working men in St Pancras, 'those unorganised mendicants' he scoffingly describes them, characterisitically downplaying his work. But in another letter his motive emerges: 'I am to meet a man about some lectures to working men in connection with my St Pancras District. It is good to have an interest not entirely selfish.' This last thought expressed the belief at the root of his whole philosophy. He had summed it up in a letter to his mother a year earlier: 'The true and only solid interests one can have are interests in others; to act otherwise is to spend not time and strength, but one's soul in a struggle for successes that lose all value as soon as they cease to be hope and become facts.'

This was the idealist, who believed that the lessons from his own life would be meaningless unless they were translated into broader action for society. The outer man, though, might present a different image. Catapulted into a world dominated by scions of the upper class, the young lecturer often found his best protection in sardonic humour. We glimpse this, and the discomfort it could cause, in Emmie's diary. Emmie recorded a remark of his which jars on modern ears as much as it evidently did on hers, for she remembered it: 'We have had a succession of rainy days [this was during the Baird Ventnor holiday] . . . caused it is said by the Gulf Stream, though why I cannot tell – because as Mr A.L. Smith would say "women have not sufficiently enquiring minds".' Here we hear the voice of male chauvinism and its public-school training ground in which A.L. had spent most of his life. We shall see how the 'divine idolatry' he felt for Mary during their courtship could later, under moments of stress, give way to this more abrasive side of his personality.

But he had a multitude of friends to whom he gave and from whom he received unquestioning affection and loyalty. His letters to Mary team with their names. There were his one-time undergraduate colleagues (we meet them again at the wedding – Norman Pearson, who went with him to London from Trinity, and Philip Gell, a Balliol history scholar); the semi-professional acquaintances with whom he enjoyed a warmer than official relationship, like the Cohens (the father a QC) whose son A.L. was coaching, and his older ex-Oxford acquaintances of the Jowett generation, among them Archibald Tait, one-time Fellow of Balliol and Headmaster of Rugby, now Archbishop of Canterbury. A.L. was in fact 'vice-best man' as he calls it for a college friend who married at the Archbishop's country house in December 1877. ('I went through my arduous vice-best-man duties including a speech, dancing, and acting to an audience of about 100 strangers; made friends with Mrs Tait, steadily but delicately chaffed the Archbishop, found a good many friends, kept moderately sober, and finally confided my opinion of "the old boy's" character and appearance [Tait was 66 at the time] to a girl who in return confided to me the fact that she was his eldest daughter,' he wrote to Mrs Baird. He could be sardonic at his own expense.)

One person who had early conceived a liking for him to the point where she virtually made him a member of her family was, as we have seen, Martha Crossley (Aunt Frank). Charitable works, an active public conscience, was part of the Crossley way of life. It is possible that Martha's initial interest in A.L. at about the time his stepfather died and he was leaving school for Oxford came under that heading. Martha and his mother had been friends and it is reasonable to assume she would have been concerned for the parent-less teenager. But it is also clear that duty fairly quickly turned into liking and liking into affection. A.L. was invited to the Crossley home in Halifax, and then to Somerleyton. There he was treated like a favourite nephew: his clothes were mended, new ones bought, no complaints made when he was late for breakfast. Then, as his teaching expertise grew, he became tutor to the Crossley's son, Savile.

In his first years at Balliol, though, he was very much on his own. It is possible that social unease, in the upper-class world of the Balliol junior common room, drove him to work even harder than he would naturally have done. He also threw himself into sport. Both led to success in the same year, 1873, when he got a first in Greats (after his first in Mods two years earlier) and rowed in the Balliol Eight which came head of the river. Thanks to the inclusion of history in the curriculum, an innovation that Jowett, Master of Balliol from 1870, had fought for, after his classical finals A.L. switched to history. He did the three-year course in one, getting a second, and in the same year won the Lothian university essay prize. The next step was a two-year college tutorship in classics; then in 1874 he was appointed to a seven-year open fellowship at Trinity College. He was there when Mary and the Brintons made their Commem week visit to Oxford in June 1877.

His decision to quit university in mid-fellowship because of the celibacy rule must have been a hard one. He was heart and soul a teacher; the university was his world and already his close relationship with Jowett had given him a glimpse of what could be done if you were in a position of power. But the lessons of the harsh nursery were not forgotten. If he wanted to marry, he had to find another way to earn his living. He enrolled at the Bar, left Oxford and set up in lodgings in South Kensington. 'I am sorry to leave Oxford, where the work is so congenial,' he wrote to his mother, 'if I had two hundred a year of my own [I] would spend a year in study abroad and then come back to teach here, instead of involving myself in the "nice sharp quillet of the law" in London. But a Fellowship that is stopped, and with it one's definite career, by the comparatively innocent process of marrying, is not a fair thing to depend on.' There is no evidence that he was already thinking of Mary. But he was a man who needed to be in control of his life. This was a sensible step.

So he moved to lodgings in London, in Alfred Place, South Kensington. It was from there that he would walk to Teddington to visit Savile's cousins whom he already knew well from their Somerleyton visits, arriving windblown and muddy after

crossing Wimbledon Common and Richmond Park. At first it
was assumed by Emmie he came for her – he was for ever lending
her books. This match, between Emmie and A.L. Smith, was
one that John Forster Baird perhaps favoured.

The two men had got on at first; in fact John Forster Baird
had gone to stay with A.L. in Trinity where they no doubt
discussed his plans for the Bar. The Bamburgh holiday of 1877,
however, changed all that, as we've seen. It is also possible that
during that holiday, A.L.'s first experience of Bamburgh, he was
at his most prickly. He did none of the things John Forster Baird
enjoyed: shooting, sketching (in fact his Strutt background
might have given him a certain contempt for the gentleman-
watercolourist). Moreover, after eight years in Oxford he would
have approached the history-rich northeast coast of
Northumberland from the standpoint of a professional
historian, unlike the Bairds for whom it was primarily
playground and romantic family roots. (Significantly, Emmie
reported going to Holy Island for the first time during this
holiday: local sight-seeing was clearly not part of the usual Baird
programme.) Above all, A.L. was a new kind of person in the
Baird world. He had never known a day's financial free-wheeling
– even in Somerleyton he was earning his keep. He knew he had
to live by his wits; his self-confidence was rooted in academic
achievement. He could be an inspired talker, but that also might
not have endeared him to his host. One story of his which was
handed down the family and never ceased to thrill me as a child
was of A.L. as a young boy meeting an old woman who in her
youth had danced with Bonnie Prince Charlie – a hop-skip-and-
jump encounter that makes history shrink. One can imagine
A.L. capping a Baird account of the distant family links with
the Jacobite Forsters with this dramatic little tale and perhaps
not being liked for it.

It was predictable, therefore, that after the engagement had been informally settled John Forster Baird would still fight a rearguard action. The stages of the affair were as follows: permission to write to each other, amounting to an informal understanding (this was secured after A.L.'s letter setting out his career prospects); formal consent of parents, leading on to the third stage, public engagement. The first, letter stage was a way of getting to know each other. We have Mary's and A.L.'s letters, sometimes two in one day (in those days one could post a letter in the morning, get a reply in the afternoon and send an answer to arrive the next morning).

The letters chart the evolution of their relationship, A.L.'s literary style contrasting with Mary's immediacy and expressive underlinings. Neither can believe their luck. Mary, faced with his 'infinite passion of reverence and fealty and tenderness' (A.L. to Mary) can hardly believe it is really addressed to her, that it is possible for anybody to love her so much. She, smarting from a critical mother, longs to be loved as much as he, after a lifetime without close relatives, longs to have an object to love. You feel the perfect balance of need between them. He is lightheaded with love: '[I] dream of you all night and carry you about all day. . . . In one day has come like a flood upon me that divine idolatry which is to be my motive force and the well-spring of my spiritual being all my days till death.' Mary, in answer, felt 'so happy, and so sure that I love you' that she was beyond caring what her family might think; she knew that they would come to love him in time. In a pencilled note she adds: 'I trust you with my whole soul to be true to what you have said and done, whatever you may hear for a few days or a week; and believe in me who never cease to think and always think of you as true.' A couple of 'detrimentals' might still be lurking; was Mary afraid of Teddington gossip?

But A.L. was above jealousy. It was a time of total and unalloyed happiness for him as his other plans too fell into place. Not everybody, however, could share the couple's joy. We learn from the letters that Emmie was morose; and Emmie, after she had extracted Mary's secret ('It is *actually* A.L. Smith!') confided her distress in her diary: 'I was never so astonished, I could almost have wept, I would rather it had been *anybody* else. . . . When will Mary cease wounding my too sympathetic heart with her innumerable flirtations? . . . My long cherished romance is over.' But Emmie being Emmie she soon recovered and turned into a valuable ally, the inevitable go-between between jealous father and determined daughter.

Mary was confident 'Somerleyton' would win her father round; which in the end it did – and not only Somerleyton. The Crossleys enlisted the help of the top Brinton, Aunt Mary, wife of the redoubtable John ('Aunt Mary is just a little too sagacious', Mary comments suspiciously). Family wires were buzzing. Mary derived piquant enjoyment from the inquisitive concern of their Teddington friends, even when it meant a three-hour visit from the vicar. But by the beginning of December she had a ring, and by their birthdays (hers on December 3rd, A.L.'s a day later) they were formally engaged. Papa had given up.

But the Bairds made one condition: A.L. should have a check-up with a doctor – after all, he had had recurrent rheumatic fever at school. So to Sir William Jenner, son of the great physician and a 'swell' in his own right, he went; and Jenner, after 'punching and pulling and listening pronounced me a perfectly healthy subject as strong as a lion', A.L. wrote to Mrs Baird. (One wonders how Captain Griffith would have got over that little hurdle.) But the couple still faced a long engagement. It was another 18 months before his plans finally came to fruition and the moment he had waited for arrived.

In April 1879 he wrote to his mother that he had been offered 'a great opening in the University for the teaching of Modern History, which I have plunged into heart and soul'. This was a history lectureship at Balliol, the signal for the longed-for return to Oxford. Jowett had written him a glowing reference 18 months earlier ('He [A.L.] is one of the best young men of his generation at Oxford, gifted with uncommon abilities of the practical sort. I have the greatest respect for him and believe that both in character and attainments he would be a catch'). Then, with the lifting of the celibacy rule, Jowett had earmarked him for the Balliol job.

His future was set up; and in the wake of the Oxford appointment the marriage could be arranged. The date was to be June 25th 1879. Mary spent early June in Oxford. The couple were fixing up their future home in Crick Road. (Martha Crossley was paying for the house lease and furnishings and during that visit aunt and niece stayed as before with Jowett.) Mary travelled back to London by train with Robert Browning who also had been staying at the Master's lodgings, a lively journey throughout which the poet stood up and talked at and over her, to the diversion of the whole compartment.

Meanwhile Woodlands was busy with wedding preparations. Wedding and bridesmaids' dresses were made by a Mrs Knight of Kingston, and Mary and Emmie would walk across Bushey Park for fittings. Emily Baird was going to wear ruby velvet (which Emmie described as 'stunning'). Fifty people were expected to the wedding breakfast, more to the evening dance. On Sunday June 22nd A.L. and Louisa Richardson arrived, while Mary held her last Sunday school class. She had continued teaching all this time, though her letters to A.L. make only one reference to her classes (and none to religion). Religion would come back into her life and never lose its central place, but during this period it recedes.

Emmie described the wedding day in her diary: 'It was at *11.30* in *our* Church [St Peter and Paul]. The Vicar of Highgate [Mr Trinder] married them, Mr Ram [Vicar of Teddington] was there, and a *crowded* church. Mary was not in the least nervous beforehand – during the service and at breakfast she only looked a *little* pale – and was *perfectly* lovely, the sweetest bride anyone had ever seen. She looked so happy then, and as for him, he was radiant.' Mary had breakfasted in bed waited on by her sisters ('the "attendant nymphs"' wrote Emmie). By mid-morning all was ready; Emmie, Kitty Brinton and Charles Strutt, an uncle of A.L.'s from Australia (known by A.L. as 'the solitary relation') went in one carriage, Emily Baird and the other children in a second one, John Forster Baird and Mary in a third. The wedding party then processed up the aisle to the 'Wedding March', Dolly and the three-year-old Daisy (as the youngest of the family was now known) bringing up the rear. Sunlight streamed through the windows while the marriage ceremony was performed (Emmie 'heard Arthur and Mary's voices *most* distinctly, especially hers, low and clear. She had a red spot on each cheek at first, but otherwise she did not seem nervous.') The party emerged from the church into a thunderstorm and a hail of rice and flowers thrown by bystanders ('Mr Pearson and I got a good share of rice!' Emmie reported. 'It ran down the back of one's neck very uncomfortably!'). At the wedding breakfast there were speeches by the vicar, by A.L., by the best man (Pearson) and the Australian uncle. The last two were missed by Mary and Emmie, who was helping her change: the bridal couple had to get the 2.30 train from Twickenham for Oxford where their honeymoon was to start. True to form in this eccentric family, when the bridal photograph was taken later on the steps of the house, the nuptial pair were missing, along with Emmie, their parents, Savile and his mother: they were all seeing Mary and Arthur off on the train. The result is a picture which shows the rump of the wedding party – younger bridesmaids, officiating clergymen, servants and various guests – but none of the main participants. The married couple also missed the evening dance.

It was to be a boating honeymoon, the same journey that they had made that Oxford summer two years earlier, with A.L. doing what he liked best, rowing, while Mary steered. Unlike two years earlier, they would take days off for detours and visits to friends. They would not be back for a month. 'I feel "dumpy" when I think of not seeing Mary for so long,' Emmie wrote in her journal.

The aftermath of the wedding in fact left the family in Teddington with a sense of loss they found hard to comprehend. It was an exceptionally wet July. John Forster Baird took refuge in complaining about the weather: 'Papa is always talking of the ruin to crops and farmers, until one feels the workhouse near!' The family's revenues were not looking good. Did it worry John Forster Baird that his rich sister-in-law was footing the bill for the young couple's new home in Oxford? Mary seems to have gone into this marriage with only that promised £150 per year, a useful but modest nest-egg.

Emmie, characteristically, would not let herself mope for long. 'I must really settle to regular employment now [July 7th] and shake off idle fancies: – weddings, I find, have rather a bad effect on one's mind!' But why, she asked, did other people have so much 'real happiness' in their lives that was denied to her? In her low mood her thoughts returned to that earlier loss, 'the dreadful stunned feeling, the misery, the coffin. . . . Oh my Doty, can it be five years since then? The grass is green over your grave.' Another separation triggered memories of the earlier one.

The happiness shared by A.L. and Mary was apparent to all when they returned at the end of July. Emmie described how she and their neighbour Jack Barton rowed downstream to intercept them on their way from the Kingston Regatta: 'At the bridge we sighted a faint vision of pink and blue far down the river [i.e. Arthur's striped red Balliol shirt and Mary's blue and grey frock]. They looked so nice in their dear little light outrigger, M steering and he sculling.' Mary was sunburnt, full of talk and laughter. Three days later Emmie noted how calmly happy she seemed to be, adding, 'But yet – I don't quite like it . . . . A and M are the most outwardly undemonstrative couple I ever saw . . . but I rather like that.' Her confused feelings about marriage and sex show through these contradictory comments. Mary was in a different league now. It was hard not to feel left out. After a night sharing the same room with her, when A.L. had gone ahead on the second lap of their honeymoon, Emmie's sense of deprivation focused (like that of Dolly, Daria Andrayevna, in *Anna Karenina*) on Mary's ravishing new dressing-gown. It seemed to sum up the differences between them and wrung from Emmie this cry from the heart: 'Oh! Oh! what *shall* I do without her?' The lopping off of first one member of the family, then another, albeit in different circumstances, made the reduced family circle seem very bleak. There is no record of what Emily Baird felt. One suspects her Mrs Bennet-like sense of satisfaction was bolstered by relief at having handed her difficult eldest daughter on to someone else.

The young couple were off to Canterbury where A.L. had to examine the King's School Balliol candidates. They stayed with the headmaster, and dined with the cathedral dean and his wife. From the perspective of a century and a half later the Trollopian world of the cathedral close seems to sit ill with A.L.'s reputed humanism. But the old-boy network of school and university had given him many a churchman friend, not only the retired archbishop. The Darnells of Bamburgh might suspect him of atheism, but whatever he felt in his heart of hearts such an extreme position would have been death to his academic ambitions. His mentor, Jowett, was a model of tolerance. It was an example he could only follow.

Their future Oxford home, 7 Crick Road, had been bought three months before the wedding but would not be ready till the summer. It had seven bedrooms, four sitting-rooms, a basement, conservatory and garden, the ideal Victorian family house in which, even in a lowly paid academic's family, a minimum of two maids (at £12–£14 a year) and a cook was regarded as necessary. Problems of housekeeping, though, were in the future. That summer the pair were fêted. Mary, in her wedding dress, on the arm of the host of whatever house they were visiting, was a sight to dazzle. ('None of you children are a patch on her,' A.L. would tell his daughters in later years.) For the Victorian bride beauty was as good as a dowry – better, perhaps, in a place like Oxford with its ambivalent attitude towards visible wealth. Mary's looks and sparkle complemented A.L.'s powerful intelligence. As they walked under the gas lamps of autumn Oxford, Mary with her wedding-dress train draped across her shoulders, they were moving into uncharted territory: a new relationship and new career, in a new home where (until the gas-fittings had been installed) they stuck candles in bottles and Mary supervised the preparation of conger-eel cutlets for A.L.'s freshmen pupils. She felt at ease in such moments of informality, unlike the occasions when A.L.'s senior colleagues and their wives entertained them. Then she would feel daunted, she wrote later, by 'that demi-semi sort of attention, with eyes on the other end of the room', with which they responded to her.

Her Oxford life had begun.

14   *An End and a Beginning*

And as the fervent smith of yore
Beats out the glowing blade . . .
So sits the while at home the mother well content.
    Robert Louis Stevenson, quoted by Mary in her Life
    of A.L.S.

Mary wrote two accounts of their first years of her marriage. One is in her biography of her husband, published in 1928, four years after his death, in which she quotes the lines at the head of this chapter without a trace of irony. The other is the diary she kept at the time, between December 1882 and March 1883.

They tell different stories. One is a memory softened by the patina of later events: the richness of college and family life, the whole weight of a 46-year marriage which produced nine children and, by the time she wrote the biography, seven sons-in-law, one daughter-in-law and ten grandchildren (another 17 would follow). The other account, in her diary, shows her at three points in time, on her 27th birthday in December 1882, three weeks later and then three months later. The book gives the general picture; the diary the look inside, under the lid. And there is a third piece of evidence: a note on the back of an envelope, scribbled in May 1882, which takes us further into the heart of Mary. Although one might ask which of these is the true picture, the answer is, they all are. Drama and fiction give us distillations of what we fondly think of as the truth. We could write a play about Mary's miserable year in 1882 (because she was miserable then) and it would make a poignant story of an unhappy Victorian marriage. But it would be an incomplete picture.

The young married couple threw themselves into college life – in a sense were thrown, by Jowett. He had sized up A.L.'s teaching skills. These could be used to good effect – as they had been with Savile – to 'drill into shape the backward but interesting sons of his numerous friends' (according to Mary) before getting them into college; it would also be a source of extra income for the Smiths. They were detailed to take young Lord Weymouth, son of the Marquess of Bath, on a reading holiday abroad during their first long vacation. It was the first time A.L. had been abroad. Baden-Baden was chosen, a place already well known to Mary (and the site of Granville and Mabel's flit in Gertrude's *Dorothea*). There was only one problem: Mary was about to have a baby. 'That presents no insuperable difficulty,' she reports Jowett as saying with glorious bachelor disregard for her comfort. So, she duly gave birth at the Villa Marx, Baden-Baden, on August 19th 1881 after a four-day labour. The German nurse, handing over her baby (a boy) said: 'You will live to have many more, my dear!'

There ensued a surreal scene. John Forster Baird and Mary's sisters had decided to go to Baden-Baden too; and Donald Trinder, the one-time Teddington vicar who had married her and A.L., was also there. On September 12th the whole crowd of them attended the baby's christening in the English church, Mr Trinder officiating. Mary's world had not waited to be invited – it had followed her.

Two people were missing: her mother and the youngest sister, Daisy, who by then was four. The year after the wedding Daisy had developed paralysis, diagnosed as polio but more likely to have been tuberculosis of the spine. Whatever the cause, she was disabled to the point where she would spend the rest of her life in a wheelchair. Because of her illness, the Bairds had decided to leave the Thames Valley and move to higher ground. Hampstead (Fitzroy Avenue) was the choice, probably because their friends the Trinders were near.

So the old home had gone. This gathering in their former Black Forest haunts was the last family jaunt of its kind. There had been Christmas at Somerleyton, with the usual parties and skating on the marshes, but this reunion in Germany had a special significance. The move to North London had not been for Daisy alone. John Forster Baird's health was failing too. Hampstead may have symbolized to him what Kensington had been to his father, a more hopeful setting for the fight against the family disease. Mary's departure had hit her father hard. There is a sketch of his, of Bowmont Hill in the Cheviots, the place he had always defined himself by ('John Forster Baird, of Bowmont Hill, Northumberland'), done on October 4th 1879, four months after Mary's marriage. The date is significant; it would have been Gertrude's 21st birthday. It seems he painted or drew every year on her birthday, building up a visual memorial to her. But this last one is a faint echo of a sketch, a panoramic view of the valley by an artist for whom the pencil has ceased to work its magic.

He died in March 1882, two weeks after the birth of Mary's second child. Because of the arrival of the baby (Gertrude, as she was called), Mary missed his death. In her diary, written nine months later on her 27th birthday in December 1882, she recalls their last meeting:

Papa has been taken from his anxious, unsatisfied life on earth to rest in peace with Gertrude [he was buried in the same grave in Teddington parish church] – he died last March 15th after 3 months illness, and I could not see him again, as my baby was only a fortnight old. My memory of him stands out vividly. He is standing in the dining room while I say goodbye to him, the old wistful look upon his face (oh Papa, how you hungered for our love, and how we grudged it to you, and now we cannot tell you of it – dear Papa, but I think some understanding must have passed between us during those last unconscious days!) And he did want me to stay on, and my heart stretched and yearned after him, and yet the old reserve blocked up the way and paralysed my tongue. Dear Papa, if only I could feel sure you knew it all now. But oh, daily and hourly I long to see and speak to him once more – he did love us, and it is death. I can speak of this to no one, but in all my pleasures I miss his pleasures and bright approving look, and maternal fondness – Like as a father pitieth his own children – so is he pitied and cared for now by the Lord that redeemed his soul.

Mary sought solace in religion. Arthur, she says, does not understand her 'higher feelings', and she is awkward in explaining herself. Will she ever be able to win him to Christ Jesus, will there ever come a time when 'against his own opinions he should be convinced'? One by one her props – father, faith, children ('Arthur did not want any') – seem to isolate her. She is happily married 'as far as earthly happiness goes' but then come sad bottomless moments when 'the old lonely feeling comes back'.

These three diary entries chart her descent into depression. The last entry tells us its causes: the death of her father as she was recovering from the baby's birth, a scarlet-fever epidemic in Oxford which infected her (mildly) and terrified her for the children, an attack of Bright's disease (kidney infection), then pleurisy in December, when she started her diary, followed by a miscarriage three months later.

It was quite a package. A.L. in the meantime was getting deeper into teaching and other university activities. There were more lodgers (among them a character called 'Jock' Wallop who helped disinfect the house during the scarlet-fever epidemic), and A.L. was appointed to a junior proctorship which meant supervising and enforcing student discipline. At the same time he took on the duties of Poor Law guardian, an elected office which involved interviewing claimants, fixing levels of poor relief and intervening in cases of extreme hardship. This was in essence social work, and his motive for doing it on top of his teaching would have been that 'interest in others' which he had written about to his mother six years earlier.

Mary would later develop her own interest, in baby clinics which she set up in the slums of Oxford. There were in each of them great reservoirs of energy which would be released once they reached calmer times. But this third year of their marriage found them, like that earlier couple, Henry and Martha Brinton, Mary's grandparents, locked in a temporary impasse of maladjustment and stress.

Hear Mary, in May 1882, in a pencilled cry of distress on the back of a letter from Auntie Jane in which the latter had discussed Mary's mother's state of nervous collapse since her widowhood (another worry):

Let me examine myself – My only confidant must be paper. How can I please him. I ought not to let him be overbearing, rude and selfish without telling him so. – I want guiding. . . . I have been cross I know, still nothing that I do is right. I wish I could see my way, but I can't. Sneering and sarcasm perpetual sicken me and now that it is public I feel ashamed of him. I had the makings of a happy wife. . . . Domestic happiness . . . will never come now.

But they went on to have another seven children. They went on, he to become a great and loved teacher, head of a college, co-founder of the Workers' Education Association, she to run her baby clinics and her huge family. And she continued to hold the tiller very firmly. My father, four decades later, going to her to find out when it would be convenient to ask the Master for the hand of their daughter, was told not to disturb him – he was very busy with university business and, said his future mother-in-law, 'I often don't tell him things like when the cook's leaving and when the cat's had kittens.' The engagement of the youngest daughter was clearly low on the list of her priorities, after the kittens. My father was delighted.

Emily Baird recovered. She came to live in north Oxford with Daisy, and took to cycling round the meadows at the edge of the growing town. In 1885 Emmie married E.T. Cook, the journalist and later editor of the *Pall Mall Gazette*. Together they wrote a *Highways and Byways* guide to London and Emmie went on to become an author in her own right, in spite of that early lack of formal education. She wrote *The Bride's Book*, which *The Lady* distributed and described as 'wise, witty, grave on occasion, but for the most part irradiated with sparkling humour and informed with practical commonsense'. Next came a guidebook, *London and its Environs*, and a collection of short articles, *From a Woman's Notebook*. This last, which came out in the year of her death, contained some moralistic stories worthy of Gertrude's tract-writer in *Dorothea*, but also several critical essays which give a very different picture of Emmie. Here, for instance, is her view of Ibsen: 'To the large majority of comparatively healthy-minded people Ibsen can only do unmixed good, by opening to them a new world of profound psychological lore hitherto undreamt of.' Ibsen's women, she noted, were 'even in their bad phases, so much stronger and more sympathetic than his men'.

Emmie had come a long way since the days when, daunted by her ignorance, she had dreaded leaving the schoolroom. Her marriage to E.T. Cook was extremely happy. They had no children, but Emmie took Mary's family to her heart and the eldest Smith daughters relished going to stay with their elegant London aunt, happy times that were cut short by her early death in 1903.

Auntie Jane took up residence in the King's Mound at the end of her life. Typically, A.L. was not informed of her inclusion in their family life. 'Who's that singing the Te Deum in a cracked voice in the early morning?' he asked at breakfast one day. But by then he and Mary had clearly defined and mutually respected territories. Auntie Jane joined the cohort of unannounced visitors (which could include an ailing baby in a basket in front of the fire) making up the accepted pattern of their life. A.L. always worked with the door of his study open to catch the children as they passed. Having not wanted any, he revelled in them once they had passed babyhood. From then on he would bring them into his world of ideas – tales of the past, dreams for the future – and his love of sport. If it was too wet for hockey in the garden, why, there was always the first-floor landing.

All of them, except Emmie and her husband, are buried in the cemetery of St Cross Church, Holywell, Oxford, my father too (he and my mother were married there). If anywhere is the family church it is there, though the attachment to Bamburgh, where my mother is buried, still remains and is in some way on another plane.

As I walk in the wild garden that the Holywell graveyard has become, I imagine a resurrection scene like the one Stanley Spencer painted in the mid-1920s of the churchyard in his native Cookham, with its village inmates stretching as they uncurl out of their graves beside their halo tombstones. The Holywell graves today would open onto a jostle of roses and wild flowers, far from the symbolic arum lilies and neat white daisies of Spencer's imagination. Auntie Jane would show her head, then Emily Baird, Mary and A.L, stirred from their sleep by rumours of how their story has been taken out of their hands.

Faced by their puzzled frowns and indignant disclaimers, I would say: 'Well, I did my best. I'm sorry if I got any of it wrong, but I loved doing it – and I'm going to miss you all.'

Appendix

Sources and Acknowledgements

The text of this book is based on a variety of sources, published and unpublished: John Baird's account book (1816–44); Henry Brinton's letters to Martha Gardiner (1817–21); John Forster Baird's continental travel journals (June–August 1846, July–August 1847), his sketches and paintings (1844–82), and his *Bradshaw's Illustrated Handbook to the Tyrol* (1863); the Baird/Potts family letters (1840s); Mary Baird's journals (October 1872–February 1874, April 1876–October 1877, December 1882–March 1883), her letters to A.L. Smith (October 1877–June 1889), her *Life of A.L. Smith* (John Murray, 1928), and her undated fragment 'How were you educated?'; Emmie Baird's journals, (March 1874–December 1874, June 1876–July 1879); Gertrude Baird's novels (fragments), *Baroness Eugenie* (1872) and *Dorothea* (1872–3), her sketches (1872–3), and letters from school (May 1875–April 1876); Louisa Richardson's letters to Mary Baird (April–July 1876); A.L. Smith's letters to Mary Baird and her parents (October 1877–June 1889); Madame Collinet's letters to Mr and Mrs Baird (March–April 1876); Laurence Irving's *The Successors* (Rupert Hart-Davis, 1967); and Rowy Mitchison's essay 'An Oxford family' in *A.L.F. Smith*, edited by E.C. Hodgkin (privately printed, 1979).

My thanks are due to my family and friends for their encouragement and help, particularly to my cousin Edward Hodgkin for transcribing Mary's and Emmie's journals, the Mary–A.L.S. correspondence and Louisa Richardson's letters.

Index